RISK TO BE HEALED

The Heart of Personal And Relationship Growth

BARRY VISSELL M.D.
JOYCE VISSELL R.N., M.S.

Ramira
PUBLISHING

Risk To Be Healed: The Heart of Personal and Relationship Growth
Copyright © 1989 by Ramira Publishing,
P.O. Box 1707, Aptos, CA 95001   408-429-9311

Printed in the U.S.A.

First printing   April 1989   5400 copies
Second printing   November 1989 10,400 copies

Cover and book design by Josh Gitomer.
Typesetting by Polaris Publishing, 125-A Alhambra Ave, Santa Cruz, CA 95062

Photo credits:

Cover photo by Mark Tucker, courtesy of Awakening Heart Productions,
5914 Channel Drive, Santa Rosa, CA 95409 707-539-3535
Back cover photo by David Weisbach, P.O. Box 1171, Monterey, CA 93942

Copyright material as follows:

White Eagle quotes courtesy of White Eagle Publishing Trust; *The Prophet*, Kahlil Gibran, © 1973, used by permission of Alfred A. Knopf, Publishers; quotes from *A Course in Miracles*, courtesy of The Foundation For Inner Peace, Inc., © 1975.

Every effort has been made to trace and contact copyright owners. If there are any inadvertent omissions in the acknowledgments, we apologize to those concerned.

Library of Congress Catalog Card Number: 88-063725
ISBN: 0-9612720-2-3

Acknowledgments

We wish to express our gratitude to our secretary, Beth Holland, for her word processing, proofing, and strategic support; to our team of editors, John Astin, Maggie Harris, John Hansen, and Nancy Ricossa, for their insightful help; to our daughter, Rami, for contributing her joyful artwork; to Josh Gitomer, for his sensitive cover and book design; to Bobbi and John Hansen, for computer page layout and constant encouragement; and to our daughter, Mira, for singing sweet songs to keep bringing us back into our hearts.

WE DEDICATE THIS BOOK
to all those beings,
seen and unseen,
who have realized
the joy and fulfillment
of taking
"risks to be healed."

Contents

RISK TO BE HEALED

Risks

To laugh is to risk appearing foolish.
To weep is to risk appearing sentimental.
To reach out for another is to risk involvement.
To expose feelings is to risk exposing your true self.
To hope is to risk despair.
To try is to risk failure.
To live is to risk dying.

But risks must be taken,
because the greatest hazard in life is to risk nothing.
The person who risks nothing,
does nothing, has nothing and is nothing.
He may avoid suffering and sorrow,
but he simply cannot learn, feel, change, grow, love or live.
Chained by his opinions, he is a slave,
he has forfeited freedom.
Only a person who risks is free.

AUTHOR UNKNOWN

Foreword
by Hugh and Gayle Prather

THE PHRASE, "you can't judge a book by its cover," implies that essence is in content, not in form. However, in the example of a book, content is not so much in the words of the text as in the part of the author's mind and heart from which the words came. The reader bathes in the inner quality of the writer. This is why it is possible for a cleanly crafted book to leave one feeling quite dirty, while very unprofessional jottings can sometimes leave one feeling clear and pure.

We love to immerse ourselves in any book written by Joyce and Barry. For us to read even a few pages of what their hands have perfected and their spirit has so beautifully brought forth is to begin to feel the presence of God. And also to feel their purity and boundless love for their readers. In this book they offer the priceless gift of their own experience with relationship, commitment, vulnerability, sorrow and loss, along with a profound guide to healing that comes from the core of their being and blesses us with gentle wisdom.

Since this is a book on healing, we would like to repeat here a few concepts that we have expressed on other occasions, concepts that we feel are sometimes overlooked in the "new age," (although certainly not overlooked in this book) especially in the one area of physical healing. In our opinion the great mistaken assumption that is currently being made is that physical healing is a change for the better. It is believed that part of the body is healed and part is not, and we know the difference. Most of us have very silly and arbitrary definitions of sickness because we judge sickness as undesirable and unnatural and even as an indication of inadequate spiritual effort. Consequently we want to avoid all signs of it and to limit the category that can apply to us. Red and swollen eyes from the flu are illness. Red and swollen eyes from "a little friendly competition" are not. To have food poisoning is to be sick, but to take offense and infect one's mind with grievances is not.

In *Notes On How To Live In The World...And Still Be Happy*, we tell about the time we were at a party in Santa Fe and a man with a shaved head (and therefore not bald), who had arrived on a mammoth Harley hog, nodded at Hugh's bandaged forehead and said, "Dirtbike injury?" "No," Hugh said, "I had a small tumor removed." We watched the man's features drop as fast as his opinion of Hugh.

But why should a lesion from a dirtbike injury indicate a more manly character than a lesion from a surgeon's scalpel? Why should the mind be somewhat proud of a leg injury from a marathon or a karate practice and somewhat embarrassed by a leg afflicted with bursitis or gout? By general agreement one is illness, the other not, and no one claims to "heal" joggers or bikers. And yet we know from our own past personal addiction that jogging can sometimes be an isolating and selfish activity, very much in need of healing, whereas the only saint we have ever known had crippling arthritis and possibly had transcended the world because of it.

Conditions that fall within people's notion of illness are believed to be in *need* of healing, and once they are changed to fit their current picture of health, the healing activity is stopped. A *judgment* is therefore dictating when healing efforts begin, the target at which they are directed, and when they have accomplished their goal. In other words, when a wrong body is set right it is healed. This motivation ignores *the effect on the mind* of a preoccupation with change — either making it or not making it.

More than simply a plea for "healing the whole person," we merely recognize that no one can see *in advance* what changes are needed or what bodily conditions are best. If this one point were accepted, then why the healer can heal at one time and not at another would not be so hopelessly confusing. When the body becomes the major concern of the mind, the mind cannot fulfill its potential. Healing, if it is to have any lasting effect, must serve the mind and not be a tool of judgment, comparison and classification.

If our highest duty is to follow wholeness, peace and the kindness of our being, to treat others fairly, and to help where we *can* help, then the condition of the body is only meaningful as it makes concentration on love easier or more difficult. Healing is therefore accomplished through love and *is* love. And love is the uniting principle in all healing approaches — in so far as they truly heal. Healing's opposite is judgment, and any system (or person) loses its effectiveness to the degree that it becomes a charge against innocence. The pronouncement that cancer is caused by an inability to love, or that colds are a lack of joy, or that AIDS is a manifestation of sinful-mindedness would not be made in the first place if we had not already judged illness as wrong. What has been accomplished in seeing that the individual plays his or her part in "choosing" a particular physical condition if it is assumed that the choice is bad, weak or spiritually inferior?

When one turns one's thought to God (to one's source, to life, to truth), a shattered mind can be restored to wholeness. And what greater healing could there be than this? When one turns one's thought to God (to oneness, to innocence, to love), the soul can be purged of bitterness. And what greater healing could there be than this?

Many people can only turn to God when they are very sick, some only when they are dying. It took an unsuccessful operation for terminal cancer with an aftermath of unending pain, for Hugh's mother to have her first deeply transforming spiritual experience. She told him that shortly after the operation she could look back on the world and see how meaningless are the concerns people embroil themselves in. She was happy and at peace, and she somehow knew that she could either "stay" or "come back." Her choice was to return and heal the relationship with her son whom she had abandoned as a young boy. And this she did even though she was disfigured and in increasing pain until she died two years later.

We cannot believe that it would have been better for anyone including herself if, instead of having the operation, she had been "healed" of the cancer. To have the slightest contact with her during those months was to feel the presence of God. She became another person, one who was open, happy and utterly unselfish, one who could and did heal the hurts of a lifetime.

Dr. Gerald Jampolsky tells a similar story at the end of *Teach Only Love*, and includes several first-hand accounts from people whom Mary Aberi profoundly affected in the period she was in extreme pain and dying. "It was as if God was speaking through Mary," wrote one woman who knew her during her final year.

What constitutes the work of a lifetime and who is to say what physical condition will help or hinder its completion? The true healer merely gives the gift of healing but does not watch over the patient to say in what form it is to be received. Not so strangely, this approach frees the healer to heal wholeheartedly, unhampered by anxiety over possible results. Where there is anxiety there can be no love. One of the fifty "principles of miracles" stated in *A Course In Miracles* is, "Miracles are expressions of love, but they may not have observable effects."

Healing must become a part of an overall program of deep inner growth, so that healing, like conscious breathing or chanting or praying or service or any other yoga, becomes merely a way of opening the heart to Being, to Love. We have one friend who heals at the moment of the client's greatest and purest inner effort. This man heals with his hands and he arranges that the client's eyes are closed so that this physical change (often a release from pain) is experienced inwardly and as an outgrowth of the client's determination to forgive, to commit, to bless or some other loving act. He demonstrated his approach to Hugh (in a hotel lobby!) and Hugh had no sense of anything being done *to* him, of anything but his own efforts (in this case to commit to the happiness of one of our sons) causing the change.

Many individuals are capable of creating an atmosphere in which the patient can change his or her unconscious beliefs, but goodness is not a necessary component at either end. Although the bodily changes we call healings are not the automatic result of bringing the mind into accord with ultimate truth, they are the result of changing the mind. For example, if one *believes* that to experience the peace of God will change a particular physical state then, quite naturally, this is the result. Belief, however, is not primarily conscious and simply saying that one believes, or trying very hard to believe, or conscientiously following a prescribed course of mental imagery, verbal arguments, mystical or religious invocations, movements, silences, sounds, etc., will not necessarily change one's deeply held unconscious belief, as probably most readers of this book have experienced for themselves. Very few of us are in a position to know — with complete clarity and understanding — our own or another's unconscious beliefs. We therefore do not know perfectly what we are trying to change or even when we have changed it. All we can do is to concentrate on healing the dark, damaged, fearful images within our *own* minds. If the results do not *look* like a healing, we need to avoid the all too common trap of blaming either ourselves or another. The instant our mind begins attacking, true healing becomes impossible because we have betrayed our calling.

To *truly* heal, to deeply and permanently affect, to transform, the mind must have no goal but innocence — to see it and to be it. To accomplish so great a feat the mind has to shift away from mere pictures and beliefs to the quiet, still knowing that is love. Harmlessness, absolute and complete, is the ultimate power. When we immerse ourselves in harmlessness, what to say and what to do is gently known. And the mind that sees itself as whole and another as sick, unquestionably requires healing. True healing is thus expressed within the mind and heart of the healer and not within the body of the patient. When a healer sees that he or she is not separate from the patient — and only love holds this vision healing is already accomplished. The mind that no longer struggles to contrast itself with another but looks happily upon its oneness with all living things, has moved into that level of reality where healing is a constant. The healer has now received and accepted the only thing that can be given away.

One of the loveliest and most complete statements of healing we have read is a poem written by Helen Schucman, the scribe of *A Course In Miracles*. We will summarize and end with it.

To heal it is not needful to allow
The thought of bodies to engulf your mind
In darkness and illusions. Healing is
Escape from all such thoughts. You hold instead
Only a single thought, which teaches you

Your brother is united with your mind,
So bodily intrusions on his peace
Cannot arise to jeopardize the Son
Whom God created sinless as Himself.
Think never of the body. Healing is
The thought of unity. Forget all things
That seem to separate. Your brother's pain
Has but one remedy; the same as yours.
He must be whole, because he joins with you,
And you are healed, because you join with Him.

Introduction

OW, TAKE A RISK TO BE HEALED," I said to someone in one of our workshops. I had said those words a number of times before, but this time the thought struck me: "What a great book title, *Risk To Be Healed*."

It was about four years ago, shortly after publishing *The Shared Heart*. We were witnessing the healing power of risk-taking in our counseling and workshops, and I was eager to begin writing about this. Sharing this with Joyce one day, she looked at me sweetly and said, "Barry, there's another book that needs to be written first."

"What's that?", I asked.

"A book about children, parenting, and family life," was her response. This turned out to be *Models of Love*. "*The Shared Heart* was largely about the relationship process," she continued. "Parenting is the next step. Here we are with small children, having so recently experienced the richness of babyhood. It's all so fresh in our consciousness. We have been learning so many spiritual lessons. I feel we need to share them now, rather than wait any longer."

I reflected on the truth of Joyce's words. But still I felt attached to writing *Risk To Be Healed*. I felt a twinge of disappointment at the thought of postponing this book for a few more years. Then my title hit me once again: "Risk To Be Healed." Here I was excited about all these other people taking healing risks, while an opportunity was dangling right in front of my nose. I knew my "risk to be healed" was to let go of another one of my attachments. Joyce smiled as my face relaxed into an expression of acceptance.

How often we expect healing and risk-taking to be something glamorous and exciting. The quiet, seemingly mundane risks we take in the course of our everyday lives, like letting go of attachments, or overcoming a habit, or appreciating someone when we would rather not, can bring about just as much growth in our souls as the more visable or obvious risks. This book is filled with examples and stories revealing the wide spectrum of healing risks.

It wasn't until after *Models of Love* was finished that we understood a major reason for waiting to write this book. Our experience with Anjel, our third child and spiritual helper, taught us so many deep lessons about healing and risk-taking. These form the first chapter and a significant part of this book.

Risk To Be Healed is definitely about healing, so we need to ask ourselves: what exactly is healing? Healing is the process of becoming whole. It is just as much a way of life as it is a goal or end result. It is an entire life process of fulfilling all our potential, becoming all that we can be. It is being and becoming at peace with ourself and with the world.

Healing is the harmonizing of the dissonant frequencies within us. On a guitar, for example, each string plays its own note, has its own frequency of vibration, but resonates in harmony with the others. When one string is out of tune, none of the sounds from the instrument are harmonious. Tuning the string creates an integrated harmonious sound.

Similarly, thoughts, feelings and attitudes can vibrate out of harmony with the rest of our being. It is interesting that many of us believe more in the possibility of physical healing than in healing other aspects of our lives. We have little difficulty visualizing a broken arm mending or an infection resolving, but we may easily feel hopeless in the face of relationship problems or perhaps what we feel has been an unhappy childhood. In every workshop, we see that psychological, emotional and spiritual healing follow the same laws as physical healing, and are within the reach of every sincere heart. We have watched numerous individuals and couples take healing risks to overcome their perceived limitations.

Healing requires taking responsibility, and this can be either active or receptive — but not passive. It is always a process that happens from inside out, rather than from outside in. Healing is not something that happens to a person. Rather, it is something that arises within a person. It is important to know that everyone is completely and ultimately responsible for their own healing. It may be active, such as doing something that needs to be done or stopping a process which has been causing disharmony. Or it may be receptive, which means choosing to allow a healing process. Receptivity is not the same as passivity. It requires courage and humility to receive. Both active and receptive healing require the taking of a risk: stretching limits or opening to new possibilities.

Now what about risk-taking? Why is it that all healing involves the taking of risks?

Truly, we can choose to spend our whole life trying to make each moment, each day, as easy, comfortable, and secure as possible. We can choose to travel only on paved roads with a carefully-planned itinerary clutched tightly in our hands, always knowing from where we have come and to where we are going.

But life is not like that. When we try to control life and resist taking risks, our souls stagnate. When we refuse to venture onto new roads, the light of spirit within us begins to dim.

The voice within our hearts is ever urging us forward into newer avenues of expression. Each day presents us with opportunities to expand our minds, hearts, and souls. However, we are never given guarantees that these new roads will be without bumps and pot-holes. And we want guarantees that we will not be hurt, so we're reluctant to leave the old well-worn path. We don't realize that bumps and pot-holes only shake us up and allow us to change and grow. How often we misinterpret this "shaking-up" as pain, and limit a growthful situation by labeling it as suffering, and hence something to be avoided.

We are all in need of healing. Our earth experience is like a schoolroom with new lessons every day. We need to accept that life is a continual process of healing and growing and becoming more and more beautiful, more and more aware of the love within us. Every time we take a risk in the name of life, in the name of God, in the name of growth; every time we take a leap of faith into the unknown, we are healed in a deeper way. We can then progress to the next level of awareness, and raise the vibrations of the earth itself. Every step we take is a step for the whole human race and sends ripples of love throughout the universe.

Barry and Joyce Vissell
Aptos, California
Summer 1988

CHAPTER 1

Anjel…Our Risk to be Healed

The Risk to Listen

ET'S TAKE LIFE EASY NOW," Barry remarked as we received the first copies of our second book, *Models of Love*, from the printer . It had been quite a challenge to finish the book while both our children were small and being homeschooled. I nodded my approval as Barry further commented, "Surely we can slow down now and make life simple and uncomplicated." "No more challenges for awhile," I thought as I sat hugging our new book to my heart.

Then I remembered a prayer I had made over a year ago. I asked that I never stop growing. I had sensed a very deep healing that I was needing and had asked for help. However, now I felt that I'd been through enough growth for awhile. I just wanted to relax.

Our family, Barry and I, Rami, age ten, and Mira, age four and a half, packed up our old camper and set off for the mountains. Never had we needed a vacation more. On the third day of our camping trip I was sitting alone when I felt the distinct presence of someone beside me. I knew this sensation well, for the same experience had happened to me shortly before we conceived both Rami and Mira. At first I felt in awe of the greatness of this being beside me, whom I could not see with physical eyes but could feel within my heart. "Maybe this is a helper," I thought, and then the message came:

"I am your third child and am ready to be conceived."

It was the last thing I wanted to hear at this time in my life.

"No!" I stammered, "I don't want to get pregnant. I don't want anything different right now. I just want to rest."

I felt this being smiling at me, loving me fully and offering the gift of its presence in my life.

I reflected on how I have always loved children. When I was ten years old and baby-sitting young ones, I made up my young mind to devote my life to children. When adults would ask me what I wanted to "be" when I grew up, I would always answer in the same way: "I want to be a mother." And motherhood *has* been one of my greatest joys in life. Barry and I have also found that part of our work with couples has been helping them overcome their resistance to becoming parents. Oftentimes I amusingly call myself a "born-again mother," as so much of my spiritual life began to unfold the moment Rami was conceived and continued with Mira's presence in our lives. During a workshop in Seattle, when I was enthusiastically expounding on the joys of parenting to a couple unsure of wanting children, a man remarked to the group, "Joyce gets a commission for each baby she places here."

With my inner eyes I have seen and felt the greatness of the souls now coming to earth. My heart rejoices at their beauty and spiritual strength. They are great peace-makers who have come to help this planet. It is a great blessing to parent one of these shining souls.

Once again I was drawn back to the presence beside me, "You can conceive me in three weeks. Your family is now ready for my presence in your lives."

"No!" harshly echoed through my being.

Where was that "no" coming from in me? For the first time in my life I was feeling strong resistance to having another child. My rational mind argued that we were both forty years old, too old to be having more children (though I knew this wasn't true). Rami and Mira were finally old enough to go with us on great adventures or else stay at Grandma and Grandpa's house while we did necessary air travel.

Barry and I had felt long ago that our family was complete, and had gotten rid of all the baby things.

I felt this great being stretch out its hands in blessing and in love, seemingly amused by my obvious struggle.

The next three weeks were extremely confusing. We left our peaceful camping spot and flew east to my home town of Buffalo for several talks and workshops. Each morning upon awakening I felt the loving presence of our third child. Each morning I would then sit in meditation and watch my crazy mind resist. The more I resisted, the more love I felt poured upon me.

Finally, when my mind had come up with perhaps a hundred reasons why we should not have another child, this message came into my heart: *"Your risk to conceive me is your risk to be healed...trust in the perfection of God's plan."*

Against all that my rational mind was telling me, the voice within my heart grew stronger and steadier. I knew I needed to take a big risk and listen to my heart, the will of my God-Self, and ignore my resisting mind. God's will for us was to conceive our third child.

Joyce wasn't the only one struggling with resistance to having another child. Our family felt *very* complete to me, too. In addition, it seemed that our work in the world was blossoming. A child at this time in our lives meant (to me) giving up the talks and workshops as a form of service. It meant nesting once again. I knew in my heart that I didn't want to enter lightly into having another child. I knew I wouldn't want to just plug a new baby into our busy, full schedule of activities. I prayed often at this time for guidance, for even a hint of what to do.

In my deepest listening, the word that kept coming to me was "surrender." But surrender to what? I wasn't feeling the "knocking on the door" that Joyce was. I wasn't even feeling the desire to have

---

another baby. So how could I surrender to something I wasn't even experiencing?

The answer came one day in a quiet loving moment alone with Joyce. It was my greatest risk, my greatest leap of faith, to surrender to the guidance coming through Joyce. I had to let go of the little boy part of me stubbornly "wanting to do it myself"...even the part of me that wanted to understand what was happening. I had to accept my unknowingness.

At last I felt a wave of peace come upon me, that unmistakable feeling that tells me I'm on the right track. I realized I wasn't surrendering to Joyce in the sense of giving my power away, the archetypal struggle of all little boys with their mothers. Rather I was surrendering to God's will, to a plan I wasn't comprehending at this my current stage of development.

It became clear to me that, given the experiences Joyce was having, we could *only* conceive a child if it was for our highest good. My great risk was simply to trust the perfection and goodness of the universe...to trust God.

I shared these thoughts and feelings with Joyce. The peace was contagious. The missing ingredient for her had been *me*. Up to that moment it had seemed a one-sided struggle...a decision which was hers alone. Now we were together accepting the gifts of God — in whatever form they might come. If a soul was to come into our lives in the form of a new baby, it was of course a gift. *We would be given the highest way to serve God, for that was our highest desire.* If it meant giving up the talks and workshops for a few years, so be it. Something better would replace that activity. If it meant continuing this form of service, then the baby would be comfortable traveling. Whatever happened would be just what we needed, as it has always been in our lives. We may not have always gotten what we've desired, but we have *always* gotten what we've needed.

A Leap of Faith

Our prayer before uniting our bodies was to serve God in the deepest way, to grow and to be healed. Three weeks of intense struggle brought us to this point of complete surrender to God's will. With this surrender came an indescribable feeling of peace and well-being. Our minds can never comprehend the fullness of any life situation. Only by becoming inwardly still and listening to our hearts can we be rightly guided.

Three days later Barry and I said good-bye to our sweet girls and to Grandma and Grandpa and journeyed to England where we attended a five day retreat at the White Eagle Lodge. It was during this time that we both saw the full glory of the soul that had chosen to come to us as our third child. We felt so honored to have been chosen as parents for this one. As we became immersed in pregnancy for the third time, gratitude filled our being. I realized that this child was coming in answer to the prayer I had been saying for over a year. This one was coming to take us a *big* step further along our path. This was a step we could only make with help. Through the presence of this one in our lives, we would both experience a deep healing. The risk to conceive our third child was like a leap in faith which was already reaping rewards. My mind still occasionally doubted the wisdom of our action, yet my heart knew that we were right on track.

When we returned to California with the children we told them of the new family member. Both girls became ecstatic upon hearing the news. The baby was due on Rami's eleventh birthday and Mira's fifth and a half birthday. Plans were immediately made for a water birth. Excitement grew!

With the excitement came an unexplainable feeling that this child would teach us about death. Barry and I tried to push the feeling away, thinking it was probably just a fear. However, it came all the more strongly. I had an uneasy feeling that this baby would never grow to be an adult. My fear told me to have an amniocentesis. My heart told me to trust. I trusted and I waited. Then severe nausea set in.

The second, third and fourth months of pregnancy were extremely difficult. I was nauseous every minute of the day, having to spend most of my time lying down. There were times when I felt so discouraged by physical symptoms that I wished I would just die. It was during these times that I tried to remind myself that a great prize — the presence of this great being — was certainly worth the price of these months of hardship. But the nausea was so severe that I couldn't really feel the soul of our baby. The knowledge that the light surely follows the darkness kept me living each new day of this difficult initiation.

By four and a half months of pregnancy I began to feel alive again in my body. I felt as if I were being born again into a new life from a period of death. The light was so bright. The baby began to grow within me and touch me lightly with its movement. An abundance of beautiful pregnancy dresses came from many loving sources. I felt vibrant, wonderful, radiant. I walked with confidence and joy, so happy to be carrying our third child.

Our little rented house underwent a major transformation as we squeezed out a small corner for the baby. Barry, Rami, Mira and I had endless discussions on each family member's role in the care of the new baby. We were all excited in anticipation of this major change in our family. Each of us held the secret hope of another little girl, and all but Mira felt that a boy would be just great too. Five-year-old Mira wanted a sister. She rationalized, "We have all girl toys. Why buy more toys?" I knew she wanted to share her special dolls with the baby.

We found a midwife at about the fifth month of pregnancy. Though we hadn't had a midwife with the first two pregnancies, we both felt a desire to have more support this time. She would examine me and be of support for Barry as he delivered the baby. I had hesitated asking this woman, as she was extremely busy with a full-time job as a nurse mid-wife in the hospital and rarely took on home-births.

Joyce and I decided to ask this woman at a house-blessing of mutual friends. There were many people present, and she was sitting on the grass when we approached her. We bent down and greeted her with a hug. After a few minutes of conversing, Joyce asked her if she would consider helping with the pregnancy and birth. She looked at Joyce, smiled, and said she would have to think about it. Just then, our attention was diverted by other friends approaching and more greetings.

The next day, our midwife-friend called. She first asked us if she seemed to have acted strangely at the house-blessing, because she wanted to apologize. When we assured her she didn't, she told us what had happened. She said that when Joyce asked her to be her midwife, a bright light appeared around Joyce and she heard the words, "of course you will." She felt almost in a state of shock and barely managed

Risk To Be Healed

to mutter the few words that she did. This had never happened to her before, and she felt deeply moved. She felt the presence of our baby reaching out to touch her...really to choose her. From then on she felt this presence, this soul, blessing her life as well. She had no choice but to be our midwife.

During her first appointment with Barry and me, the midwife could not hear the baby's heartbeat with her regular stethoscope. She felt we had no need to worry as the presence and spirit of the baby was so strong. Often it is hard to hear the heartbeat at that stage with a regular instrument. Arrangements were made to meet again after Christmas for another check with a more sensitive instrument.

I was confident and assured that the baby was fine. Each day I rose early to meditate and asked to feel our baby's presence. Each day this presence was there stronger and stronger, not only assuring me that it was very much alive within me but also gently guiding and instructing me. These mornings with our sweet babe became so precious to me. I was receiving a deep spiritual training.

Several days before Christmas I was filled with the realization that our baby was female and that her name was Anjel (Ahn-jél). Anjel ... Anjel...the name filled me like an affirmation. I felt bathed in her presence. Each morning I woke with a sense of ecstasy at the glory of her being. "Oh Barry," my first words of the morning would be, "her very essence is so beautiful. We are so blessed." Barry would smile and share my joy. I knew he was also concerned that I hadn't really grown much bigger in a month. He was looking forward to the next visit with our midwife and finally hearing the heartbeat.

The day of our appointment came. My meditation and time with my sweet "angel" was very special. As expert hands felt my uterus, concern crossed her tender face. "Joyce, you haven't grown. I want you to have an ultrasound test to determine what is happening."

Barry made the appointment immediately and off we went with the children. As we drove to the hospital Barry explained to us that this test would let us see the baby's movement and possibly determine why she didn't seem to be growing this last month. As I waited in the office while Barry and the children went to register for me, I reached into my purse and pulled out a little package of "Angel Cards." Each of the fifty cards has a picture of an angel with a corresponding word. The card I

Anjel...Our Risk to be Healed

chose was the angel of *gratitude* — reminding me to be grateful for all that I am given, knowing it is a gift from God.

Stretched out on the x-ray table I gathered the children and Barry close as the technician began scanning the uterus. Sadness etched her face and her professional manner faltered. In one of the most awful moments of my life, she announced, "Your baby is dead." Rami and I burst out crying. Then the radiologist repeated the test and called Barry outside. Little Mira looked pale and confused. Extreme grief filled my being and I was all set to jump into a tunnel of darkness when Mira spoke, "Mama, I'll take a boy rather than no baby at all. Will that help?"

Her innocence and purity touched my heart and I smiled. In that moment, I knew that I was to be grateful for my two healthy children, rather than mourning the little dead body inside. I remembered the angel card of gratitude and sat up and hugged and kissed the children. I felt so much love for them and the precious gift of motherhood. We hugged each other and cried. Barry returned to the room. All four of us cried together and were grateful for the love we all felt.

I remembered my meditation that morning, and the assurance that was given that she was very much alive within me. That thought caused the most grief. "Why?" my mind pleaded. "Why such assurance when this physical proof was revealed?"

Barry called an obstetrician friend and another immediate appointment was made. The process was begun to remove the dead fetus. Surgery was set for the following morning.

Lying in bed that night, my body ached from crying. I lay in a state of sadness. Unable to bear the sound of Barry sleeping, I woke him and said, "I need some wise words." He sat up in bed, rubbed his eyes and tried to wake up. He gently rubbed my back and tenderly smiled. I so dearly love Barry's fatherly smile. "Why was I given so much assurance that the baby was alive?", I asked. "Is my intuition all wrong?" I needed the answers to these questions.

Risk To Be Healed

Being awakened in the middle of the night and sitting up in bed with Joyce, I ordinarily would have been groggy and sleepy. So I was surprised to find myself wide awake and alert, as if I had been meditating rather than sleeping. I was also surprised at how easily the words flowed out of my mouth and heart:

"Your intuition could never have been more right. Anjel has always been alive within you. You were connected to the vastness of her being and presence, far more than to the physical body in your womb. That's why you have looked and felt radiantly pregnant, even though the little body was not alive.

"Anjel never needed to be born in a physical way. Her greatest need was to give her love to the world through us. This she has been doing all along, but this pregnancy has deepened her link to us. *The creation of a physical body has anchored her consciousness within us both.* It has been a tremendous leap for all of us.

"Beloved Joyce, Anjel has been born within us. We now have three children, two with physical bodies and one with a body of light. We have just as great a responsibility with our third child as with the other two. We are parents to Anjel in the sense that we are caretakers for a more evolved consciousness. We have the joyful responsibility of maintaining our connection with her. The work she will be doing requires that connection. In addition, we are like children and she our mother. We now know a spirit guide, a being who is holding us in her loving embrace while she works through us."

These words helped us both that night, as well as in the difficult times in the months ahead. They were meant just as much for me as for Joyce, for I had been worried for a month. Not every day and not seriously, but still it was there. It started the moment our midwife felt Joyce's belly and listened with her stethoscope. I felt and listened too, and although the doctor in me said, "probably too early — nothing to worry about," I felt an uneasy feeling that something was just not right. The midwife looked over at me, tuned right in to that feeling I was trying to bury, and did her best to assure me there was nothing to worry about. Although that feeling never really left me, I would only have to look at Joyce to see the picture of a healthy pregnancy. Even though her belly wasn't growing, the radiance of her face and body were telling me, "Barry, how can anything be wrong in the presence of all that light?"

The next day, December 30, 1986, we went to have the D & E (Dilation and Evacuation, a procedure for removal of the dead fetus). Our obstetrician advised general anesthesia and inwardly we got the go-ahead. We prayed together for Joyce's protection and for the doctor's hands to be blessed and used as instruments of healing. Then Joyce was led away.

Out in the waiting room, four very dear women friends and I sat in a circle holding hands, praying and meditating. Every once in a while, one of us would speak a prayer or some inspiring words for reflection. I have never participated in a more one-pointed, concentrated healing circle. Joyce later told us she felt held in loving arms the whole time.

In the beginning we were tested by two women sitting very close to us, gossiping *very* loudly and unaware of what we were doing, although it seemed obvious to us. As I was sitting, trying to hold a deep concentration, some loud negative comment about a third woman would catch my attention. I started wishing they would become aware of us — or leave. I had the thought to start singing but dropped that idea. Then I thought of getting up and politely asking them to be quiet. I decided against that, too. Finally, I became amused at how funny it all was — the stark contrast of our energies. I realized they had a purpose in being there too. Those two women were forcing us all deeper in our concentration! I started feeling grateful for their loud gossip, blessed them, and returned with renewed vigor to our healing concentration. Within minutes, the two women got up and left. Their role in that scene of the play was over. Could they have been angels in disguise?

After an eternity, I opened my eyes to see our obstetrician beckoning me into a little room. Joyce was not awake yet from the anesthesia, but he wanted me to know all was well. He told me the little body was female, and then asked if I wanted to see it. I did, and followed him into another room. He went over to a counter, took the lid off a container and reached gently inside. Before taking the body out, he turned to me and warned me that it wouldn't be the prettiest sight...

I was prepared to see a fetus somewhat shrunken and macerated from lifelessness in the womb. But I was *not* prepared to see a face that reflected the timeless wisdom of the ages, a face that was in every way ancient, yet so completely devoid of life, just like an empty shell. I stood there looking at this face and body, holding it in my hands and more deeply understanding the mystery of birth and death. Then the door opened and a nurse called my name. Joyce was awake and I hurried into the recovery room to be reunited with my beloved.

That evening we went to bed after setting the alarm for 3:45 a.m., so we could be awake for the first world peace meditation to be held worldwide at the same hour. In California it was to be 4-5 a.m. At exactly 4 a.m., while we were sitting in bed, neither of us feeling very peaceful or inspired, the door to our room slowly and quietly opened. We knew it was Rami (Mira could not yet open a door quietly). She poked her head in our room and whispered, "I have an earache!" Joyce and I looked at each other and smiled. Joyce then turned to Rami and said, "Rami, you don't have an earache. You're just feeling what's happening right now all around the world." Rami's face relaxed and she said, "I guess I really don't have an earache." She smiled. Rami had been awake lying in bed and at 4 a.m. had felt an urgency to be with us. She knew she needed a good excuse to wake her parents up in the middle of the night. We're convinced her ear gave her a momentary twinge of pain to provide the necessary excuse.

Sitting in bed for that next hour, the three of us felt so happy to be together. We clearly needed Rami in that hour to help us. And help us she did. We so strongly felt Anjel's loving presence in the room, giving us deep assurance of her nearness and the gifts she was bringing into our lives.

The Love Behind All Appearances

Three days after the removal of Anjel's body we were scheduled to give a workshop on the Hawaiian Island of Oahu. Since I was physically unable to travel I decided to stay home with my visiting parents, and Rami and Mira. I would join Barry in several days for a small vacation and rest before we started a seven day "Training of the Heart" workshop.

The morning that Barry left, the milk came into my breasts. My body was confused and was producing milk for a baby. This was perhaps the hardest part of the whole experience. For three days I walked around with breasts tender and full of milk. As painful as this was physically, it was nothing compared to the pain it brought to my heart. Nursing had been such a highlight in my mothering experiences. It was almost more than I could bear to now have the milk and no baby to receive it. In this period of despair, Anjel's presence came to me all the stronger. Through her love she gently took the pain away and eventually the milk went away too. I never felt alone.

On the third morning of Barry's absence he called from Hawaii. I burst into tears upon hearing his voice. I missed and needed him so much, and wanted desperately to talk with him. The connection was very poor and I could hardly hear him. He finally managed to communicate that he'd call me during a lunch break in the workshop. That time came and went. There was no phone call. By late evening I realized there would be no phone call. I felt terribly hurt and in my extreme state of vulnerability all of my old insecurities began to emerge. I was convinced Barry was off in Hawaii having a grand time, totally oblivious of the pain I was experiencing. I pictured him laughing and joking, totally happy to be away from my tears.

I started to feel anger. I was scheduled to leave the next day to join him and didn't even want to go. As I felt anger and distance from Barry I could no longer feel the beautiful presence of Anjel. As soon as I had separated myself from Barry, closed my heart to him and saw him as a hurtful, inconsiderate person, I could no longer feel the incredible grace and love from our baby. During the next several painful hours in which I battled with my feelings of anger and hurt, I realized I could only come back into feeling the grace of our baby's love when my heart was opened to all beings, especially to Barry. It is through our love for each other that she came to us originally, and it is only in feeling that love for each other that we will continue to receive her blessing.

Upon going to sleep I started feeling my love for Barry once again. Warmth and tenderness filled my heart as I thought of him. "How much Barry really loves me," I thought. With that thought came a beautiful vision of Anjel. It was as if she were standing in the room, smiling upon me with a radiant glow. With my inner ears I could hear her sweet message to me, "Let your attention always rest upon how much Barry loves you. Have the courage to see past the appearance of certain actions and words, and go straight to the love within his heart.

Feel the power of that love and let nothing else become more important." From her smile and radiance I knew that she would be helping us to feel our love in a deeper way.

In our experience working with families we have learned that children's great desire is for their parents to come into a state of love and harmony with each other. Concentrating upon each other's love and devotion, rather than upon each other's seemingly thoughtless actions or mistakes, has brought a deeper level of harmony, trust and love to our own relationship.

With the vision of Anjel and her wise words soothing my mind and heart, I fell into a peaceful sleep. I woke several hours later to the sound of a phone ringing and heard my father answer, "Hi, Barry. Yes, she's been waiting for your call all evening. Now she's asleep." The phone lines had been down. Barry had tried to call. I smiled to myself as I drifted back to sleep.

The next morning I said goodbye to Rami, Mira, Grandma and Grandpa. My parents, visiting from the East, were watching the girls for two weeks while we did our work in Hawaii. I boarded the plane with hundreds of happy expectant folks all prepared for a grand holiday in Hawaii. I had to enter by wheelchair, as the operation and general anesthesia a few days previous had left me extremely weak. As I sat on the plane listening to my little personal stereo, tears flowed easily from my eyes. Each song and piece of music seemed to remind me of the joy I had felt while pregnant. My friend Margaret, whose fourteen-month-old baby had died a year previously, had warned me not to hold back tears. "Tears cleanse and help to wash away the sorrow," she wisely told me.

I wiped away the tears when lunch was brought and turned to the couple sitting next to me. They had been saving money for five years for a one week trip to Hawaii. I glanced and saw mask and snorkel sticking out of the man's day pack, ready for immediate use. Their excitement starkly contrasted to my reddened, puffy eyes.

"Why are you going to Hawaii," they curiously probed. I tried to shrug off their question with a simple reply. "I'm going to lead a workshop with my husband." However, that stimulated them even more and they asked to know the name of the workshop and what we did. I felt somewhat embarrassed, knowing my answer would confuse them in the light of how many tears they had seen me cry. "The name of the workshop is the 'Training of the Heart.' We help people experience inner joy." "Oh!," they said with a strange look on their faces. I could tell they were confused. I had to laugh to myself to see their doubt about how I could pull off leadership of such a workshop. The man finally blurted out, "How do you get people to come?" I could understand why he was confused.

As the plane was landing I remembered my one request to Barry before he left: "Please be right at the gate when I arrive." Having to be confined to a wheelchair and in my weakened state I felt so vulnerable. All I wanted was to be with Barry once again and feel his fatherly love. In eager anticipation of receiving his warm hug, I was wheeled out to the gate and left there.

No Barry! My heart sank. I felt like a small defenseless child dropped into a busy world with no protection. People pushed and shoved to greet those coming off the plane. "Aloha!," was called out again and again as flower leis were placed around necks in greeting. The people all seemed so eager and joyful. Coming to Hawaii was their dream come true. Soon the crowds dispersed and I was left in my wheelchair with no greeting or flower lei around my neck. Despite all my efforts, tears began to roll down my cheeks once more. I felt abandoned and unloved! Dark thoughts invaded my mind and anger began to rise within me. Then I remembered the vision of Anjel and her wise words to let my attention rest upon Barry's love rather than upon seemingly thoughtless actions. It took tremendous inner work to rise above the anger and fear I was feeling and to concentrate upon his love.

Finally I did it and at that moment I felt a flower lei placed around my neck by my breathless husband. "I came an hour early to be sure I'd be here on time," he puffed out the words. "Then the ticket agent told me the plane was coming in at a gate one half mile from here. I even checked the computer monitor to be doubly sure of the gate. When I realized the mistake, I ran the whole way here, but I'm still thirty minutes late." He was obviously sorry, and I realized this entire incident was perfectly orchestrated to reinforce the beautiful lesson I had received.

Wheeling me to the inter-island terminal for our flight to the island of Maui, we were greeted by three women who had been in the

Risk To Be Healed

workshop. Each placed a flower lei around my neck and confided to me that Barry had spoken so often and so lovingly of me that they had to meet me.

Two days later I was strong enough to walk again, but not strong enough to speak to one hundred twenty people, I thought, as I hesitantly walked into the Maui Palms Hotel where a luncheon with a guest speaker is held each month in Maui. Barry and I were the speakers for the month. It was now one week since the removal of our baby's body. This was the first group of people I had been with since that time, except for a small group of friends who had gathered for a memorial service the day after the operation. An old friend called out from the crowd, "Joyce, congratulations on your pregnancy. When is the baby due?"

"This is going to be harder than I thought," I groaned inwardly. I wanted to run away and turned to go back out the door. I walked right into a smiling pregnant woman. "Our babies are due on the same date," she said happily, unaware that my belly wasn't as big as hers now. (I still looked slightly pregnant)

I cannot really express in words how much I wanted to leave that room. Retreating to a little corner where I stood alone pretending to be very busy, I said an urgent prayer. I then felt surrounded by the love of our baby just as strongly as when I was still pregnant, and felt her reassurance that I would be helped and guided every step of the way. Whenever we are called upon to do a difficult task, we need to remember that there are unseen helpers by our side ready to serve whenever we humbly ask. Having gained strength and courage while standing for that brief time in the corner, I moved out into the group.

The atmosphere of the luncheon was that of a gay party. People were greeting each other again after the Christmas holidays. There was a roar of laughter, and the warm friendly spirit was felt everywhere. I settled down beside Barry to eat my lunch, hoping we could remain unnoticed. Of course that was impossible. We had many friends on Maui, and our books had always been well-received there. People greeted us with so much love and lightness. "Do you think you'll have a boy or girl?" They all assumed I was feeling as light and joyful as they were. "It's wonderful you're going to have a third child." No one except Barry knew the heaviness of my heart. "It's great how you've kept your weight down during the pregnancy."

No one knew that at any moment I could start sobbing. My heart throbbed wildly as a long and glowing introduction was given. I had never been so afraid of standing up and giving a talk before. I feared that I would open my mouth to speak and start to cry uncontrollably for the remainder of the time allotted. Having accepted my worst fear, my heartbeat slowed to a more regular rhythm. As we walked to the front of the room, people cheered and clapped. "They aren't expecting what they are about to receive," I thought.

I stepped up and received the microphone. My hand was shaking as I held it. The room began to fade from view. "Oh no," I thought, "my worst fear is about to manifest." I asked God to help me in this the most difficult talk of my life.

"I always speak the deepest feelings in my heart," I started out. "Today I hope you can bear with me through pounding heart and shaking hand as I share my sorrow as well as my joy."

The energy instantly changed in the room from the party atmosphere to an intense quiet. I told the story of conceiving Anjel and then her mysterious death after six months. I noticed people's hearts were opening in love, not only to Barry and I but to their own pain and to their own loved ones. I told them of receiving the word "gratitude" as my key in this situation and how the daily practice of thankfulness was keeping me above the storm of emotion that threatened to submerge me. And finally I told the group how living with death in the past week had made me realize how important it is to reach out and appreciate loved ones each day. No excuse is good enough for neglecting to reach out and embrace our loved ones while they are still alive. Death can come when we least expect it, so we must take every opportunity to give our love to those around us. The time is now!

Barry led an inspiring exercise on appreciation and then spoke about how blessed he felt to be Anjel's father. Our scheduled talk of thirty minutes was soon over, the most difficult as well as the most beautiful talk we'd ever given.

Soon afterwards, a man rushed up to us and told us that he could see a radiant figure, which he felt was our baby, standing over us pouring her love upon us. We indeed have a beautiful helper. Each person in the room was deeply touched.

Surrender and Vulnerability

Kalani Honua means "the harmony of heaven on earth." "This retreat spot has been appropriately named," I thought as I walked the grounds of the place we would stay for seven days during the "Training of the Heart Retreat." Fifty people had come from all over the United States and Canada to take part in our first seven-day retreat. Charley Thweatt, talented musician and beloved friend, would be helping us by providing music. There was an air of excitement as people arrived from Alaska, Idaho, New Jersey, Canada, Maryland, and elsewhere. I was beginning to forget that our baby's body had been removed ten days prior when a beautiful woman arrived who was just as pregnant as I should have been. Tears instantly rolled from my eyes as I gazed upon her. I then retreated to our private room. I knew that much of my healing during this week would come by being close to this woman and letting the memory of my pregnancy be present the entire week. This woman, and her bulging tummy, would help me to keep the presence of Anjel very much alive within me.

We began our week by sharing our story. We shared our weakness and vulnerability and how we were in need of healing as much as anyone else. More than ever in our lives we were aware of the need to step aside and let the leadership come through us rather than us doing the leading. We felt very humble as we sat before our group of fifty, whose hearts were already beginning to open in compassion and tenderness.

The week flowed more beautifully than we could have ever imagined. Beautiful healings, joy and much laughter took place. Truly God was at work training us all. Barry and I watched with a sense of awe. On the fourth day of the retreat, during our morning session the pregnant woman began to softly cry in the back of the room. As I walked to sit by her I realized how we had all ignored the very sensitive condition of pregnancy. Urging her to join in our singing, dancing and laughter, swims in the ocean and emotional releases, we had forgotten how vulnerable seven months of pregnancy can be. My response was to have all of the mothers in the room form a circle of love around her.

A man's voice offered, "Why don't we all form a circle around each of the pregnant women and give them our love?"

I hesitated. My thoughts went back to the night I found out that our baby had died. I had called my women friends. Somehow I had the feeling that, besides Barry, only women could really understand my pain. I had asked women to help me in my grief and had avoided my male friends. I had mistakenly felt that because men could never experience the particular pain of having a baby die within them, they would be unable to fully understand and therefore help. I knew Barry had that capacity because of his deep attunement to me, but I doubted that other men could be as sensitive. While I was hesitating, several of the men in the group eagerly got up and were massaging the feet and heads of the pregnant women.

Suddenly the room swam before me and I was just able to communicate to Barry that I too was still pregnant and needed help. Then my vision was blurred by tears. I cried for a long time while Barry held me and other warm and loving hands comforted us both. Charley sang and I finally allowed my grief to fully surface as I melted into a sea of love and understanding.

When I finally looked up I was surprised to see that I was being held and comforted mostly by men. Tears were streaming from their faces. They were crying with me! Their compassion was so deep and so real that we were as one being, feeling the pain and joy of motherhood. One beautiful male friend from Mt. Shasta spoke for us all: "Joyce, we all feel Anjel so strongly. We are all saddened that she did not join us physically, but we rejoice in her presence among us. Surely we are all blessed to be here together."

I hope I never underestimate the power and capacity of a man's ability to feel a woman's pain. Men and women *are* as one being, functioning in two different bodies. If we could only pay more attention to our basic spiritual and emotional sameness than to our differences, we would live in much greater harmony.

I felt so much light and love in my being. I have helped many others to come into a state of receptivity and vulnerability and thus receive the power and love of God coming through others, but I had never deeply experienced this for myself. I was extremely grateful.

When Joyce started crying I knew immediately that it would be a big one. She had completely let go of her leadership role — not just for the moment, to be resumed after she stopped crying. The response in the group was total and immediate. Everyone knows innately when something real, something big, is being released, but this particular group was amazing in its sensitivity. I'm sure that working together in such an intimate way for four days had helped.

I was standing there holding Joyce in my arms, her tears soaking through my shirt. I was aware that many from the group had gathered closely around us both, pouring their love and healing into us. I felt my heart starting to burst open, to melt into an ocean, to lose myself into a total expanse of beingness. Momentarily, I hesitated. Could I too completely surrender leading this retreat? It had often been a quality of our relationship that we could take turns leading as a harmonious dance...alternating rhythms of expressivity and receptivity. But never had we *both* completely surrendered leadership! I struggled to open my eyes and look at the faces pressed closely around us. I had the strange sensation that I was saying goodbye to all that had gone before in these days together, that whatever even subtle walls of separation existed between me as leader and them as participants was finally dissolving. Then I closed my eyes and was engulfed in a wave of blissful emotion.

It was entirely too much effort to stand up, so I sank slowly to the floor still with Joyce in my arms. I was dimly aware of sobbing and crying all around us, as if the earth herself was expressing all the pain that it had to endure through the ages. Yet at the same time it was ecstatic, for Joyce and I were being held by much more than physical arms.

Anjel was there, so much more than a baby...majestic in the power of her love. Her presence was there to remind us that we have all the help we need, that we are *never* left alone, and that we don't have to struggle in this life. If we could all just trust a little bit more in the goodness of this greater power and love, which is always there for us, then all our needs — every last one — will be met.

In that time of rapture, Joyce lay in my arms, the two of us lay in the arms of the group, and all of us lay in the arms of God. I was deeply aware of the interdependence of all life, the thread that connects every part of the universe like a cosmic string of beads. I was especially aware of my need for Joyce, for the group, for all people everywhere — all parts of God.

How often in this life I have forgotten my great need for others, holding myself aloof and distant. How often I have acted like "an island unto myself," exhibiting false pride and arrogance, pushing away the help and love which others were trying to give to me. How often I have pushed Joyce away when I needed her most.

In our first book, *The Shared Heart*, an entire chapter, "Freed Need Seeds", was devoted to need in the relationship. Everywhere we go, people ask, "Isn't need and dependence unhealthy?" And our answer is yes *and* no. Yes, it is unhealthy when one person expects another to meet his or her needs. But it is very healthy to simply be aware of our deep need for our loved ones, to accept that our need for others *is* our need for the Divine Presence. We ask people to constantly reflect on the difference between needing and demanding, and the sometimes fine line dividing these two. When we can accept our needing, our dependency, our human attachments, and just let them be, the result is peace.

Inevitably, someone in a group will ask me, "What is your spiritual path now?" They understand that ours has been a journey involving many paths, many disciplines, many teachers. Perhaps they want me to divulge some secret meditation practice, or name a particular guru I am following. I answer, "I am on the path of need and dependence. My highest spiritual practice is to feel my need for Joyce, my children, my parents, my friends, everyone and everything. When I do that, I am then feeling my need for God. I used to try to feel my need for God and push away people, but how can I feel my need for God whom I can't see, when I push away people whom I can see?"

Someone approaches, leans over and says, "The cooks want you to know that lunch is ready. What should we do?" I am lying, nursing on the bosom of God, and someone is asking about lunch. A faint part of me says, "it's lunch time, time to all get up, form a circle, sing grace, have announcements and eat. Come on, Barry, you're the leader." Then I feel my body and realize it refuses to move, my stomach isn't even slightly hungry, and all I want to do is speak loving appreciation to all those around me. My only desire at this moment in life is to love and to bless.

Someone else approaches and asks me about the afternoon schedule. "Are we meeting back here as a group? Are we going on an outing?" I looked at these two lovely persons who were simply caring for the group. I put the one in charge of organizing for lunch, and the other in charge of the afternoon program. I am no longer in charge. Let whoever wants to eat, eat, and whoever wants to go somewhere, go somewhere. I am so content to lie where I am with Joyce near me, feasting my eyes on the beauty of those around me, and speaking my deepest heart-feelings.

I look at Joyce. She is so happy, so content. Her tears have given way to so much peace. She is mothering me and everyone by her silent serenity. I am fathering her and everyone by the outpouring of my heart.

Although this peak experience, this heightened awareness and love, finally diminished, like a rain-shower of grace that finally softens, the rest of the week carried the fragrance of this moment. Of course we stepped back into leadership roles, but with a deeper knowing of who the real leaders are. Anjel, blessed Anjel, you are one of them...

"I vow to choose life, rather than wishing I was dead," was the most moving vow of the week, spoken by a fifty-year-old woman who had spent much of her life wishing she had never been born. Our week together had been profoundly beautiful. On our final night, all fifty of us felt that we had been joined into a spiritual marriage of commitment and honor to one another's growth. Though some might never see each other again, the connection of love would never be broken and would continue to be a strengthening force throughout our lives. We had shared a vision of life from the mountain top of consciousness, and merely the thought of each other in times of need would strengthen that vision.

As each person spoke their vow, we all felt an indescribable feeling of the sacredness of each human life. Each looked so precious in their desire to grow and serve God. Our hearts melted to hear the sincerity of each word. I knew that I was just beginning to catch the feeling of preciousness and compassion that our Heavenly Parents have towards us all as we strive, sometimes falteringly, on our path. Truly each soul is beloved in the eyes of God. Each attempt and each step taken is cause for much celebration in the heavens. As each of the fifty people cheered in their hearts at the growth and steps taken by their new friends, so also were our unseen helpers cheering all our efforts.

During the week, I had seen with such clarity the tremendous blessing of Anjel's brief life within me and of her continued work through us. My vow on the last night of the retreat was to live my life in a state of receptivity to her, allowing her presence to grow within me as God intended. I accepted the responsibility of our third child. Just as I strive to nourish Rami and Mira, so also will I strive to nourish the connection with Anjel's spirit, so that it will live and grow and shine through me.

Every Experience Brings a Gift

Walking off the plane in San Francisco, Rami, Mira and my mom and dad greeted us. How happy I was to see those two young bubbly faces and the two aging tender faces. Family is very sacred to us. Much of our work is dedicated to help people strengthen the bond of love between themselves and their children, parents and mates.

Back home in our day-to-day routine it was evident that my personality and body had some catching up to do with the clarity of vision I had experienced during the retreat in Hawaii. My body still ached to be pregnant, and to prepare to hold a newborn in my arms. My outer self was still very attached to the fact that I should have been seven months pregnant. Sometimes even when we can see things so clearly with our inner self, it takes time for our outer self to catch up. There was still much grieving and letting go to be done. There were many tears to be shed and much wisdom to be learned. Though I had walked several steps along the path of this experience, I was needing to walk the entire trail, with its ups and downs, to fully receive the prize of Anjel's brief life on earth. I had been shown where I was going. Now I needed to get there. The word gratitude stayed with me as my friend and companion, my joy in happy times and my key to unlocking the darkness of my sorrow.

Before my parents left for snow-covered Buffalo, my mom sat me down for a beautiful moment of sharing. I could tell she had been contemplating what she was about to say for many days. My mother understood my recent experience very intimately. Also at six months of pregnancy, twin boys had been born to her. They had only lived two days. Though I had never seen these brothers, I had always felt a strange closeness to them.

My mother began, "I was very depressed after the twins died. Even though I had your older brother Bruce, I still had little desire to go on living. Then one day I realized I had to make a gift out of this tragic experience. I looked at my life and realized I had been self-centered and closed. I decided that my gift from this experience was to begin truly reaching out to others. Now this is my greatest joy in life." My mother smiled as she spoke. I have never known a friendlier person in all my life. Each person she meets instantly has a place in her heart. Once when one of my counseling clients had called for an appointment and had gotten my mother on the phone, she asked after a few minutes if she could make an appointment with her instead!

"Now," she continued, "you can either dwell on the sadness of losing your baby or you can find the gift in all of this. Since you are my daughter, I know you'll find the gift."

It was enough. Her speech was completed. I got the message! Just when we think we know more than our parents, they come out with a gem of wisdom. It's our job as children to keep on listening for those gems.

Parenting and Being Parented

We have a favorite natural foods store in Santa Cruz where we do most of our shopping. The only problem with the store is that it's difficult to be in a hurry, since a number of friends will inevitably be there.

"I hope we don't see anyone we know," I remarked to Rami and Mira as we hurried into the store. I had fallen back into an extremely busy routine, juggling work and children. This particular day had been more tiring than most, and I had let the cold darkened sky add to my dreariness. I was on the edge and I knew it.

Wheeling our shopping cart along the dried fruit section, I stopped short. There ahead of me was a friend who had gotten pregnant the same time as I had. We had laughed together when my belly had initially grown much bigger than hers. Everyone thought I was going to have twins. Now her round blossoming eighth-month figure glowed with expectancy. Rami, Mira and I looked as she waddled up the aisle, her added weight obviously slowing her.

"Quick!" I whispered to the girls as I pulled them over one aisle to the spaghetti sauces. Alone in this tiny section of the store, I hoped no one would see us. I looked at the girls. They looked at me. And in one brief instant of recognition of a shared feeling we all three started to cry. I held the girls, they held me, and we could not stop crying. Oh how we ached inside for it all to be different, and for the joy of pregnancy to return. When someone would pass by we quickly pretended to be studying the spaghetti jars. I laugh now to think of how silly we must have appeared in our attempts to hide our tears, especially five-year-old Mira reading the spagetti sauce labels.

Finally a beloved friend rounded the corner. "I saw your car parked outside and knew I had to stop." She seemed to know exactly what we were experiencing, said the right words, and helped us through the check-out line and out to our car.

Driving home that day I knew I had to make a big change in the way I was living, to get through and learn from my remaining six weeks of "pregnancy."

"You don't have to take me to the library Mama," Mira spoke

during our family conference. I smiled. Mira loves the library. I had realized after our spaghetti sauce incident that *I* needed a tremendous amount of mothering. I decided that during the next six weeks I would love and nourish myself much the way I did for the girls when they were first born. I knew I needed quiet, peace and as much retreat from the busyness of the world as possible. Though my body was back to its normal size, part of me was still pregnant and needed to prepare for a different kind of birth.

"I'll stop everything but my ceramic class," Rami offered. Each family member was asked to sacrifice something so that I could have this time of healing and retreat. "I'll do all the food shopping," Barry smiled. "And I can handle your side of the business work for six weeks."

Finally it was decided that all the extra activities outside of our homeschool would be canceled, except of course going to the library and ceramics class. The girls and I would stay at home, having our lessons and play time, living quietly and simply. Barry agreed to take on most of my outside responsibilities. A woman chiropractor friend sent me an article she wrote for her patients. She wrote about changing all the "shoulds" in your life to "coulds." Rather than saying "I should do this today," saying instead, "I *could* do this." In my case it was mostly, "I won't and it's OK."

Correspondence piled up. Phone calls went unanswered. Duties were left undone. Rather than being down on myself for not doing my work in the world, I gave myself acceptance and was reassured that this time of nurturing, healing and mothering myself was my most important work. Barry lovingly supported me.

There are times in everyone's life when it is important to retreat from the world and either stop or cut down on outer responsibilities. We need to remember that our responsibility to our inner growth and healing is also important, and sometimes we need to devote ourselves fully to that work. People advised me, "Keep busy and you'll soon forget about the baby." Keep busy doing what? If we busy ourselves with distracting and meaningless activities we can actually delay the necessary inner healing. If we keep busy loving and nurturing ourselves, we set a beautiful healing force into motion. We deserve love and attention from ourselves. There are periods in our lives when we need to concentrate fully upon gentle, nurturing care of ourselves, making it our most important job. The *Course In Miracles* says, "When we are healed, we are not healed alone." We serve others by our efforts to heal ourselves. When we become strong we can help others to become strong too.

There was a time in 1972 when I was very emotionally upset. Our relationship was threatening to dissolve. I did not know about taking time to heal, and instead tried to keep myself very busy in work. I felt like I was going to break inside, and still I pushed myself harder. Finally there was an accident, a dog bite which infected the bone of my hand. I was hospitalized with both arms immobilized. This was the way I received the necessary time alone to heal my emotions. Other people get sick. How much better to take the time while the body is healthy to receive the necessary inner healing.

I was able to "put on hold" all of my responsibilities except one: giving and receiving love from my family. Rami and Mira and their schooling became a part of my retreat time. In times of retreat it is sometimes important to have meaningful activity to keep a flow of energy. I knew a man who stopped his work and cared for his beloved elderly father. He needed these several years of isolation while he underwent a major spiritual change in his life. Others write, compose music, study, hike, or garden. It is important that this activity nourish your soul.

For me, the most nourishing activity was being with my children. Never had I needed them more. Their joy, enthusiasm, caring and innocence were like nectar to my soul. When my arms and heart longed to be carrying a baby, the girls filled them with love. The night after the removal of Anjel's body I lay down with Mira as usual as she drifted off to sleep. Just before her eyes closed she sweetly said, "You won't be lonely, Mama. I'll let you hold *me*." We held each other a lot during this period. I held the girls. They held me. They were experiencing sadness themselves, especially Rami who had been the most excited about the new baby.

Each day after math and reading lessons for Rami, number writing for Mira, violin practice and drawing, we treated ourselves to our favorite activity — doll making. Their Christmas present had been a baby doll kit. I had thought that making a doll right before the baby was born would help the girl's prepare for their new sister. Little did I know when I ordered the kit that these dolls would be our therapy in a time of loss. The kit was composed of natural materials forming a lovely soft baby doll, the kind used in Waldorf School kindergartens. Rami made her own doll. Mira needed a little of my help.

As we worked on the dolls each day, our main lesson in homeschool began: how to deal with loss, sadness, disappointment and grief. As I openly shared my feelings, they were encouraged to share theirs. As we stuffed the head of the doll, we talked about Anjel and how her head would have been just about that big by now. We talked about how Anjel is far more than the little shriveled up body we had seen. We talked about how fortunate they were to have a special sister in the heaven world. As the dolls slowly came together, so did their feeling of love for their angel sister.

At one step in our doll-making the directions became very hard to follow. We just couldn't understand why tightly tying a string around the middle of the head would be a good thing to do. We debated, "should we skip this part of the directions because it didn't sound right to us?" Then again, the author of the directions was a master doll designer. Surely she would know what we should do. Finally Rami said, "Let's trust what she is asking us to do." So even though it didn't seem right to us in our limited vision of doll making, we tied the string. Then we were asked to tie another in a different direction. Suddenly our dolls were transformed and now had beautiful puffy cheeks and a forehead. What was once just a round ball shape, became the form of a lovely baby's head.

We then likened this to God's will. Sometimes we are asked in our hearts to do something and we have trouble understanding why. We have a choice. We can either skip that direction, or we can trust that the voice of our heart is a master designer of our life. By choosing to follow that step we find we become even lovelier than before, just like our baby dolls.

As we tenderly sewed smiles onto the dolls, the smiles on Rami and Mira's faces were genuine in their understanding of Anjel's short life, death, and continued life through the four of us.

Finally the day came when the dolls were finished! We all ran to a special drawer in the bathroom. We had not opened the drawer since the day before we found out about Anjel's bodily death. In this drawer we had tenderly placed very special newborn baby clothes for her. Now we opened the drawer in excitement. Each girl picked out her favorite outfit. Yes, they fit! What a grand moment as we paraded around the house. The girls had worked through the greatest disappointment of their young lives and had emerged victorious.

"My baby's name is Anjel," Mira said proudly. "No! My baby's name is Anjel," Rami retorted. "No! I said it first." (Why must this bickering be present at the most poignant of times?!) After a little battle it was decided that both baby dolls would be named Anjel and would sit upon the girls beds forever after as a remembrance of the blessing of their heavenly sister.

Rami and Mira were healing me and helping to bring me back into balance. The more I was with them, the calmer I was feeling. They were helping me to bring the vision of Anjel's presence into practical everyday use.

Whenever we see someone in one of our workshops who seems particularly stuck in some aspect of life, and stubbornly refuses to move on, we always ask, "Do you spend any time with children?" Usually the answer is "No." Since children are so fresh from the heaven world, they are an important link to the wisdom, lightness and love of that sphere. By cutting ourselves off from children, we are cutting ourselves off from a vital flow of life force. I strongly believe that children are among the most powerful healers on this planet.

We don't have to have families of our own to receive the gifts that children bring. A grandchild, niece, nephew, friend's child or a child in need will do just fine. The important thing is that we are around their energy, have a willingness to enter into their world, and have a desire to give to them and flow with them. By their very nature, children teach us to be flexible, to change and to grow. It is hard to be stuck in a particular mood or pattern when there is a child around constantly urging you to move, play and explore life once again. There is an oversupply of children who are in need of an adult's attention. They may be physically, mentally or emotionally handicapped children, delinquent children, children without fathers or mothers, or children whose parents simply cannot give them the attention they need. Devoting yourself to helping one of these children could be very therapeutic.

When Barry was in his first two years of medical school, his study was largely of a mental nature. Since we did not yet have children of our own, he often played games with neighborhood children in an attempt to balance all of this mental work. I shall never forget a loud knock on our door one Saturday morning while Barry was studying. Opening the door, I found six children all under the age of seven. One girl bravely stepped forth and asked, "Mrs. Vissell, can we play with your boy?" Barry did not disappoint them, and for half an hour there were squeals of laughter as he played a wonderful game of chase. He then returned to his studies with renewed vigor. Giving time to these children had been his gift to himself.

My relationship with the girls was very beautiful in this period of healing. However, Barry and I were not as close as we could be. In the beginning, the grief caused incredible closeness, but after about two months we gradually became aware of a distance growing between us. This is often the case. Grief over the loss of a child often at first brings a couple close, then later can serve to cause distance or separation.

Barry is my partner for life. After twenty-three years of sharing and relating very closely there is no doubt that we both want to live the rest of this beautiful life together. Barry is my beloved, and from the very core of my being I know that God wants us to always love each other and serve together.

Even with this depth of love and commitment, there are periods in our lives when we drift apart, and moments when we don't even like each other. As long as our minds continue to struggle or get distracted by less important things, so also will our relationships have periods of imperfection. How can a relationship be perfect when the two individuals have not attained perfection for themselves?

People are amazed to find out that Barry and I still bicker and fight, that we sometimes yell and scream and even occasionally feel hatred for each other. We've learned that this is not a symptom of the end of our relationship, but an outer manifestation of the unrest that still remains within our minds. We realize from such feelings how much work remains within us in calming our minds and emotions. In this way, our relationship becomes a mirror for looking at our own individual work. We simply cannot hide from one another.

Upon hearing of the baby's death, Barry effortlessly became the perfect loving father for me. While Rami, Mira and I sat huddled in a corner crying, he was calling an obstetrician we knew and finding out the best way to proceed with the physical details. In the beginning he was always there when I needed comforting and would lovingly hold me as I cried. Then I noticed we were together less and less in these tender times. He somehow became busier than usual. I went alone to cry, and started to prefer being with the children.

We had always gone for a walk in the evening after putting the children to sleep. This was our time together to reflect on the events of the day, to work out the problem areas of our daily lives, to share our thoughts, to laugh, or to stop for a kiss and embrace. I started making excuses for not wanting to walk at night, and Barry seemed always to be making phone calls at the time we would normally walk. Late one night (when we were tired, of course) we each blamed the other. I lashed out, "I wish you'd allow me to comfort you over your feelings of this loss." Barry retaliated, "I wish you would show as much enthusiasm and joy over my presence in the room as you do to Rami and Mira."

We realized that we had both gotten off balance. The beautiful, protecting father part of Barry now needed to be balanced by the receptive and open son. The receptive child energy that I had so deeply felt after Anjel's death needed to be balanced by loving mother energy towards Barry.

The next morning, after our meditation, Barry lay his head on my lap and said, "Will you help me to feel my sadness over this loss?" As he lay on my lap, the fatherly protector melted away into the receptive child and he experienced his own feelings of sadness. My heart rejoiced to mother and care for him as he had so wonderfully done for me. Now we were back in balance, and together we held each other and shared in the experience of grief.

Risk To Be Healed

When Joyce and I could enter *together* into the human experience of grief, we could at the same time enter into the resolution of that grief. It was almost as if Joyce had to experience the emotion for both of us, as long as I continued to deny my own human feelings. As I acknowledged that I had feelings too, we were allowed to come back into balance. And that coming into balance becomes a powerful healing force. When we are united, there is no problem that can't be worked out.

Couples can lose their balance in different ways. A prominent one is the spectrum extending from human emotion to spiritual feelings. So often one person of a couple tends to "spiritualize" their feelings too much (for example, me). Spiritual, metaphysical, or new age concepts can too often be a form of rationalization to cover up the fear of one's own emotions. The other partner, meanwhile, is often on the other side of the spectrum, which is giving too much power to human emotions. It is remarkable how the more one goes one way, the other goes the other way. Couples exhibiting this dynamic can bring balance back into their relationship by listening to one another, by remembering that one reason they were drawn together was to learn from each other. Balance comes when the understanding and feeling of emotion are both honored equally, when neither one is more important than the other.

Another major spectrum, as Joyce illustrated, is the parent-child continuum. When couples come to see us in counseling, one of the first things we notice is whether the parenting is in balance. With all too many it is not. One is more stuck (polarized) in the role of "parent," while the other takes on the role of "child." The couple's growth is stifled until the parent accepts and releases the child within and the child does likewise with the parent within.

There is a natural fluidity of cycles in a healthy relationship, times when one is parent and the other child, and then other times when it switches. When Joyce and I have our deepest moments of communion, we find ourselves taking turns being parent and child, alternating back and forth.

One of our favorite practices in workshops involves graphically illustrating this dynamic. After pairing people up, we have one become parent and the other the child. The parent holds the child just like a real parent would. The child experiences becoming vulnerable, dependent, and needing to be loved. This is a reality of everyone's inner child.

Often there are tears throughout the room as participants experience a part of themselves they had been repressing.

Then we reverse roles to give each partner the opposite experience. The remarkable fact is that each experience is contained within the other. People find that they cannot fully open to becoming a child without also opening to the inner parent. And the full experience of parenting is not possible unless the inner child is also experienced. In a way, a child creates its parent as much as a parent creates its child.

Couples can come more into balance by remembering they have a child within that needs nurturing as much as an inner parent that needs to nurture. They also need to remember that they are drawn together because of a balance that is already there. Part of the reason two persons are drawn together is to experience this balance. Men and women so often complain that their partner either can't nurture or else be nurtured themselves. They don't realize they are drawn to be with that particular person because he or she has just what is needed for that balance. Otherwise there would not be that underlying attraction. It is often a matter of taking the initiative to get past the resistance to opening to your *own* inner parent or child, rather than waiting for your partner to do it first so it will be easier for you.

So if you find yourself being the "grand nurturer" too much of the time, seek for ways to humbly reach out to your partner for nurturing. This does not mean demanding to be nurtured. It means taking the risk to make yourself truly vulnerable — and sometimes being creative about it too, seeking out new ways to let your inner child reach out for the love it needs.

And if you find yourself relating to your partner too often as a child to a parent, you need to look for ways to give love to your partner, no matter how comfortable you've gotten being taken care of by your mommy-wife or daddy-husband. Your relationship will be out of balance and will not grow unless something is done. Find loving ways to take care of your partner, perhaps even invisible ways that don't confront your partner's resistance, for they may be very reluctant to let go of their parenting role.

Create times of openness to one another to share these things, to work together on creating ways to bring balance into your relationship. Allow your relationship to deepen. Allow perfect balance to be restored so you both can fulfill the higher destiny of your coming together, the real purpose and work you have together, the unique healing you can bring to this planet.

Beyond Birth and Death

My relationship with Barry was back in harmony, the girls and I were experiencing much joy, I was loving and nurturing myself and the California sun was brightly shining. Life was good, except for one thing: I was not healed yet. Amidst my daily chores and activities, thoughts of loss would come upon me: "She's gone!" "I should have been eight months pregnant by now." "I'll never get a chance to feel her physical body move again." Where were these thoughts coming from? Each one was accompanied by a feeling of hopelessness and powerless-ness to change my situation. It felt as if a dark cloud was descending upon me at these times.

During such times I tried to relive moments of inspiration and clarity by reading from the journal I kept. I knew the absolute truth of the vision of Anjel's life and death and continued life through us, but the feeling of loss still held power in my being. I knew I had to delve into this feeling and make peace.

I arranged a day to be alone. I prayed to be shown why the feeling of loss was so strong within me. I felt guided to pick up Steven Levine's book, *Who Dies*. With enthusiasm I read the chapter on grief. From this excellent chapter I learned that we enter each life with a reservoir of grief. All of the unresolved grief from our many lifetimes are carried into this present life. Normally we are unaware of this deep pool of grief within us until something happens, like a death or painful separation, which plunges us not just into the individual grief experience, but also into the depth of the unresolved reservoir of grief.

I realized that though I had experienced the death of close friends, relatives and beloved animals, it took the death of my baby to plunge me deeply into my own reservoir of grief. The experience of Anjel's death was giving me an opportunity to look at a hidden part of myself. As I brought healing into this individual grief, I would be bringing healing into the collective grief I had stored within me.

Following a breathing practice from the back of Steven's chapter, I dove into the feeling of grief and loss. Memories were beginning to awaken within me. I remembered being a nursing student at Columbia-Presbyterian Medical Center in New York City. Their Children's Hospital was the largest in the city and held the most dying children. Working with these children was the most meaningful part of school for me. Whenever I was with them, I understood why I had gone into nursing. I volunteered and spent as much time as possible with them. One little six-year-old girl had completely stolen my heart. She was dying of cystic fibrosis, a hereditary lung disease, and was in her terminal stage. Oddly, whenever I would sit with her the experience seemed familiar. I seemed to understand her mother's pain as if I had felt it before.

Then a memory came of an experience six months before becoming pregnant. Nicholas, our friends' fourteen-month-old boy, had suddenly died. I had made several trips to visit Margaret, the mother. I brought her flowers, books, encouragement and love. I had thought I was going to lend her strength. But each time I left I was vaguely aware that God had sent me to learn from her, and that I would someday need all she was teaching me.

Then I remembered walking down the road one night with Barry while I was four months pregnant. The thought came so powerfully, "This baby is going to die when she is five or six years old. This thought had shocked me! I shared the thought with Barry, but concluded that it was probably just my fear. However, I could not quite erase the feeling that accompanied that thought, and an imminence of death had stayed with me for the remaining two months that Anjel's body was within me.

Then suddenly my memory seemed to go back beyond time and space and just for an instant I saw the most lovely little six-year-old girl. She had dark hair and dark eyes and was my beloved child. She was the only child I could have in that life time. My love and devotion for her was awesome. Then she died, and my grief over her loss was unbearable. I never recovered. The memory of that pain lingered on within me and became part of the fabric of who I am in this life. I saw how the feeling of loss in that past life had colored certain areas of my present life, and determined how I reacted to certain situations which might involve loss.

At last, I opened my eyes and was back in the present moment. The sun was shining brightly, the bird's chirping and the flowers where I sat glowed in splendor. All of nature seemed to be confirming that I had touched upon a truth. "Go deeper," the earth seemed to say. "Heal that loss and grief completely." "Be free," the wind whispered as it made a path around my body to the waiting flowers. As I watched the flowers dance, I knew I was being given a golden opportunity to dance on the path to freedom.

Anjel, I deeply believe, was the same little girl of my vision that had died at six years old. Now she came again and died after six months in the womb. The spiritual connection with her was undeniable during pregnancy and remains just as strong after her death. She is teaching and showing me that she can never go anywhere. She never left as a child of six years old. It was only my thought of loss that created and maintained the separation. She is not lost from me now and continues so beautifully to hold me in her love. As I joyfully bring her inside of me and allow her to live within me, knowing that nothing has been lost, I will be shaking and loosening a chain which has kept me bound for so long.

Each painful loss we experience, each death of a loved one, loss of a relationship, loss of a job, or loss of any kind, can be a valuable tool for healing the grief and pain that we carry from each lifetime. It is not important that we remember any of the details of a former life, with its pain, grief and joy. It is only important that we work on this present life. Each time we let go of the feeling of loss and know that nothing that is experienced in the heart can go away, we become freer. Each time we are asked to let go of a particular form, whether a person, a thing, or a situation, and trust that the love will continue, we are being given a valuable opportunity to grow. The process of letting go is a key to our unfoldment.

"I'm healed!," I shouted. The earth seemed to smile and respond to my innocence, "Not yet, sweet child, there are stones left unturned." It mattered not to me in that moment. I felt so free and fairly flew along our wooded trail. All I had to do was to keep Anjel's love alive within my heart. She seemed to smile and sing with me the entire day.

The next weekend we traveled to Berkeley to give a seminar. I shared my most recent discovery with the group. One young woman lit up in the back of the room and came forward to share her experience. She had fallen in love for the first time when she was fifteen. She had felt completely devoted to a nineteen-year-old man. Together they explored the mysteries of love and each year grew closer. After five years she felt ready to marry him and have children together. Quite suddenly the man met another woman and left their relationship. She never saw him again. The woman described her feelings of despair and loneliness over this loss. She felt she could never love again. Severe grief set in, and she saw life through a dark cloud.

One day as she was walking through the woods, brooding over the loss of her boyfriend, the thought came to her, "Where could all the love go?" She realized that the love they had felt for each other, the happy memories she had and the discoveries they had made together, were all still a part of her. As she opened her heart to the devotion she had always felt for him, she also experienced all the love they had so beautifully felt. The love was still alive within her and did not depend upon her boyfriend's physical presence. She saw this man as a teacher along her path of understanding. He had helped her to learn valuable lessons which would always be a part of who she was. She described a light which went on within her, dispersing the darkness and bringing forth much joy and freedom. She saw so clearly that as long as she dwelt upon the sadness of a loss and felt anger and resentment, the darkness would pervade her being. As she was able to feel compassion for the man, and grateful for the love that they had shared, then the beauty of the relationship would remain within her heart and serve as a beacon of light for her. She described how this beacon of light from her heart had directed her steps to her present, very nurturing relationship.

If we look only at the appearance of happenings in our life, we may feel that we are suffering loss, tragedy or even regressing in our growth. If our hearts remain open in gratitude and trust, we will soon see that the empty place is only our foot in mid-air preparing to come down another step closer to the goal of divine love and understanding.

Humility, Forgiveness and Healing

"You have more to go, Joyce," my friend Roberta smiled at me as I finished telling her how I was all healed from the experience of my third pregnancy. She lovingly continued, "There is more in there to be released. I can feel it. Please let me help you."

I knew she was right! Though I had tried to convince myself that I was all healed, I knew deep within that I wasn't. The experience still did not fully flow through me as a strength. I *wanted* to let it. I wanted to be done and moving on with the next stage of growth. As our friend Ram Dass often told us about particular blocks we had been working through with him, "You aren't cooked yet. Let the heat remain a little longer." I still had some steps to take in order to fully receive the fruits of this unusual pregnancy.

As Roberta sat nursing two month old Michael, I reflected on how her wonderful friendship had been a gift of the pregnancy. Roberta was an acquaintance, someone I had only met once. She had called to tell me that she was pregnant for the first time and had heard I was also pregnant. She was six weeks ahead of me. Then I received the phone call that she had placenta previa and that the baby's life was threatened. Placenta previa is a condition where the placenta is to some degree covering the cervix, the opening of the uterus, blocking the birth canal. There is usually bleeding, and it can result in miscarriage.

I immediately drove the hour south to see her. She was required to lie in bed for the remaining months of pregnancy. She kept bleeding and leaking fluid and each day lived with the possibility that her baby might never be born. Lying on her bed together we had beautiful talks about trusting and allowing the wisdom of mother nature to flow through our bodies. Despite her obvious concern for her baby's life, we discussed the fun we'd have together when our two babies came. There was one more visit shortly before Christmas in which we prayed together and asked God to help her little one, as her condition seemed to be getting worse.

Several hours after my baby's body was removed, her son Michael was born. He was small and premature, but radiant and healthy. It seemed our connection through our pregnancies was deeper than we both knew. As she burped little Michael, whom our family had all come to adore and whom she had made our "God-child", she urged me to set aside a time to come to her house for a "breath-work" session.

There are times in our lives when we need the help of others to heal and come into greater balance. I have usually sought for answers within or to have them come through my relationship with Barry or the girls. Then there are times when the guidance points toward a particular person, and it is our risk to go to that person in total surrender. As we open fully and trust, we are really trusting that God can use this person as an agent of healing. Sometimes people come to see Barry or me in counseling with the motive of curiosity, or perhaps wanting to hang out or socialize with us, or hoping we can magically cure them. These are never very good sessions. At other times people come with a feeling of trust and surrender that we can be used to help them. These are *always* wonderful sessions, for the person's trust just seems to draw the right words from us. There is no such thing as the perfect healer to solve your problems, but there is the perfect healing situation in which both healer and client trust in God's power to come through, for the advantage of both. When the one seeking help is willing to have an active, rather than passive attitude in their healing, they are well on the road to receiving the needed help.

I trusted Roberta's faith in God. As she had experienced the possible loss of her own baby, she was very sensitive to my feelings. An appointment was made for March 15th. I looked on the calendar. There, lovingly written on that date surrounded with hearts and flowers, were the words "Blessing Way." This was the day I had asked all of my busy friends to set aside to come to our home to honor the baby and help prepare our family for the birth, through ceremony and singing. At the time of writing it into our calendar I had felt that this Blessing Way was going to be much more meaningful than the ones with the girls. However, I had not comprehended just how meaningful this day would be.

Lying down in Roberta's office, surrounded by crystals, she instructed me in a certain breathing technique she uses with all of her clients. Then we both prayed and asked for God's help. Breathing deeply I felt Anjel's presence right above me. I felt how she was really more alive than I, for in her body of light she was fully aware of God's presence. Whoever feels more of God is more alive. The beauty of her soul made me cry. I felt how she came to us as a baby so that we could experience her touch and strengthen our link with her. To experience her being in such a personal way is something I have desired my whole life. I was vaguely aware of her presence and influence as we wrote our other two books and the tapes for pregnancy. I was all set to reach up and say, "Yes!", work through us and help us too," when a darkness came over my being and I felt filled with unworthiness. "Where does that unworthiness come from?" Roberta urged me to look at a hard place.

Then a vague memory of a far distant lifetime burst forth. Barry and I were teaching and healing together. We were given much spiritual power. Many started to come to us. Rather than remembering God, we started using the power for our own egos. Soon the source of that power was forgotten, and we felt it was our own. At the close of that life we moved on to the spirit world and were again shown the Source of all power. In that awful moment we were not judged, but judged ourselves. The experience of having misused spiritual power was so strong in both of us that we desired never to do that again. Though this memory was buried in my unconscious as with the loss of my little girl, it became part of the fabric of my being and determined how I reacted to certain situations. At many different times it kept me from truly expressing myself. It was easier to feel unworthy than to take the risk of making the same mistake and expressing myself from my ego. I remembered the care and devotion we had given to our first book, *The Shared Heart*. We had prayed over each chapter and had traveled repeatedly to Mt. Shasta, California, to receive the inspiration of that sacred place into our writing. When we were finally completed with the writing and editing we were pleased. Then it took us several months to take the risk of actually publishing it. It was during these months of gathering courage that this original memory had surfaced. We both felt that the spiritual quality we most wanted to develop was true humility, knowing always where the power of our work is coming from. We knew that publishing the book would totally change our lives and force us into the riskiest area of our lives: bringing our work into the public. Before taking that step we needed assurance that we would not be allowed to go astray again. The assurance came in the knowing that we would be unable to live in harmony with each other as long as we were off our path of humility. Our relationship would serve as a barometer of how fully we were feeling our Source. Trusting in that fully, we published the book, and our relationship has indeed served to keep us going in our chosen direction despite the many changes that have come.

Now Anjel has come to help us burn the remaining seeds of unworthiness, asking us both to open fully to her presence and help, trusting that she and other unseen helpers were working through us. The pregnancy was a sign of our worthiness.

"You need to forgive yourself, Joyce. Forgiveness is the key to letting go of that mistake." Roberta's voice spoke truth. I saw how perhaps we have all made the same mistake, that of giving our egos the glory rather than God. Perhaps this was a necessary mistake in order to understand the importance of true humility. I had always seen this mistake as something really bad, a fault deep within us. Now I could look upon our misuse of divine power with compassion, seeing it in the light of how young in soul years we really were at that time. That "mistake" had brought a sincere desire to serve God in humility.

I feel that many hold back from expressing the full glory of God because of a similar feeling of unworthiness. We have all made many mistakes, and each one can be used as a valuable tool to help us learn and grow and experience the beautiful children that we are. By the concentration on humility, knowing the true source of all the beauty in our lives, we can each be a radiant channel of God's power and love. In this present age, the teaching of divinity will not come through one or several people alone, but through many, and each one of us is needed as an instrument of that expression. Each one of us is a piece of a puzzle, fitting our individual lights together into one magnificent whole, the full manifestation of God upon the earth. In helping our brothers and sisters to shine, we are helping the whole to shine. It is through the whole or the One that our earth will be transformed into a planet of light. Each of us has a responsibility to shine God's love to the fullest. Anjel came to remind Barry and me of that responsibility and to let us know that help is always available.

I felt so grateful as I sat up and looked into Roberta's eyes. She had truly been used to help me, by uncovering a blind spot. I couldn't wait to drive home and tell Barry...

Risk To Be Healed

When Joyce came home and greeted me I knew right away that something deep had happened. There was a newness about her that compelled me to enlarge my vision, to make room for more. Seeing that I was receptive, she poured out her experience with Roberta.

As I entered into the experience of Joyce's session and her realizations, my mind shot back about four years to the writing of *The Shared Heart*. I had gone off into the woods with my trusty folding chair and notebook to work on a chapter that was slow to take off. I felt stuck, as if writing in a medium of cold molasses. On my previous writing day I had sat with pen in hand for hours. It was the writer's nightmare come true: nothing on paper to show for hours of "writing."

This day I grimly sat there preparing for another struggle, when the thought came to surrender this chapter to those who were more capable writers than me. So I prayed for the help and guidance of those dear ones who were always ready to help. And help they did, but not in the way I was wanting. Instead, I received what I thought was an inspiration for the last chapter of the book, a story about a fictitious couple who go through a series of initiations, who almost fail the biggest challenge of their life, the test of humility. The story ends with them eventually passing this test, their meeting with their beloved master, and their final mission of service to the world.

I had never written anything so effortlessly. Words fairly flew onto the pages of my notebook. And although I was conscious that this was a fiction story, I was oddly and yet completely identified with this couple.

In the years that followed, people would occasionally refer to "our" story at the end of *The Shared Heart*, implying and sometimes even stating that this was a true story. I would reply that perhaps elements were true, but that it was "inspired fiction".

Now, however, something about Joyce's experience jogged my

own memory. Yes, it was so clear! We were — and are — that couple in the story who misused divine power. We were — and are — feeling ashamed of what we did, and thus felt unworthy to be entrusted with that great power again. And we have — and will continue to have — the opportunity to forgive ourselves, to see our failure as part of a greater plan of self-mastery.

Rather than being inspired to write a story, I was given a vision of our work on this planet — past, present, and future. And this wonderful friend and helper, whom we refer to as Anjel, is and has always been an integral part of our growth process.

In one moment of realization it was like the final pieces of some great jig-saw puzzle fell into place. Perhaps Anjel's whole mission with Joyce and me was to first make us aware of the roots of our feelings of unworthiness, and then to gently guide us into the healing waters of forgiveness.

It was truly an awesome thought, yet the feeling of peace in both of our hearts as we sat there holding hands reinforced the great truth being revealed to us. Looking into one another's eyes, we took turns forgiving ourselves for the misuse of divine power, just like a mother or father would do for a child who makes a mistake because of clumsiness or lack of experience. Then we asked, more deeply than ever before, to be continually shown the way to perfect humility. As we embraced, it was as if Anjel were saying, "Don't worry, my children. Don't ever worry about being God's instruments. You will surely be shown the way."

An Inner Birth

"Joyce isn't speaking on the phone for awhile. She is preparing for the birth next week," Barry told a friend who had called. "But I thought the baby had died," was the confused response. "There is going to be a birth anyway," Barry replied as he smiled to himself.

My behavior for the next week must have baffled all but a few understanding people. I knew that I was being prepared to give birth to Anjel. Though I still homeschooled and cared for the girls, the remainder of my energy and focus was turned inward. I was being called to focus entirely on preparation for birth.

March twenty second dawned bright, warm and sunny. I hugged and kissed my family and left for a favorite retreat spot in Big Sur. Here I could have the quiet and peace needed to "birth my baby." Driving up the steep remaining half mile to the retreat I passed a lovely bench overlooking a spectacular canyon. My body began to shake. I parked my car, found my room, and began walking towards the bench. My body was shaking all over. When I reached the bench I knew why. Ten months ago I had sat at this same bench trying to write a script on bonding for pregnant women. I had labored over the script and still it was not flowing well. Then I put my paper and pen aside and started thinking of the beautiful souls coming to earth at this present time. I felt such a devotion to them. Along with this feeling of devotion, I felt a heavenly peace flow through me. I felt surrounded by the love of a beautiful angelic presence telling me she would help. I remember bowing my head and, in deepest gratitude, asking that I might always be allowed to serve this one in any way possible.

The next month I had become pregnant with the same radiant presence. It was at this spot of dedication that unknowingly I had opened to the pregnancy. Now my body shook with the desire to give birth to this being of light. I sat on the bench and watched my body shake. I felt such compassion for my physical form. It had responded to the call of pregnancy with such strength, like a full team of experts setting out to complete a task. The baby's body was then removed unnaturally, but the forces of nature within my body, my "team of experts," still had a task to be completed. Even now my body felt ready to give birth. Tears flowed as one more step in the letting go process was completed.

March twenty third dawned with expectancy. This was the day I had intuitively felt would be the birthday of our baby. I meditated and prepared for a birth. Then I lay down on the bed and slowly went into the gentle, quiet breathing I had done at my other two births. I felt Anjel above me, filled with compassion.

Then the breathing became stronger and rather than preparing to push a baby out of my body, I was preparing to receive my "baby" into my body. Gradually I felt her essence enter my body and become a part of my life and being. I accepted the fullness of her power and radiance within me. Then I felt aglow, the same sensation I had felt when holding Rami and Mira for the first time. Rather than being able to touch her with my hands, she gave me the gift of using these hands to touch others in blessing and love. Whenever I wanted to cradle her in my arms, all I needed to do was reach out and cradle another of God's precious children. Whenever I wanted to speak to her, all I had to do was to use my voice to give the gift of love to others. Whenever I wanted to receive her inspiration, I only needed to sit in silence and ask.

She was born in the very heart of my being. She touched us physically with her small body so that we would always trust in her presence, like Jesus and his disciple, Thomas. Through a constant receptivity to her, we are being set free. The essence and qualities of Anjel melted into that of our great Mother God. It is to *Her*, our Heavenly Mother, the magnificent feminine principle of the universe, that all honor and gratitude for this blessing goes. Anjel was but used as a messenger of Her wondrous love. The Great Spirit is touching us all in a thousand ways, reminding us of the nearness and protection of heavenly love that is available to all of us.

Thank you, great Mother God, for touching me with your love. I smiled as I remembered my struggle over not wanting to conceive Anjel. Her wisdom had flooded my heart, *"Your risk to conceive me is your risk to be healed."* How grateful I felt for taking that risk. I understood healing now as an ongoing process, a never-ending journey into greater joy and deeper peace. Anjel had guided Barry and me another great step along this wonderful journey of life.

Driving home the next day I felt a desire to have something of the earth, something I could touch to verify my beautiful experience of birth. When I reached our mail box there was a tape sent by a friend, Robert Frey, in San Diego. He had composed a song about Anjel and asked a woman friend to sing along with him. Listening to the tape I knew I had received something of the earth that I could always touch to affirm the reality of my experience.

In asking us to take risks in our lives, God, our Higher Self, is really asking us to enter into a healing space, a space which takes us closer to our freedom and deeper into the experience of divine love. The life of seeming security is nothing compared to the boundless flight of living in the heart.

Risk To Be Healed

Yes, I must write to my dear mother and tell her I finally found the gift of this experience.

Born in the light of an Anjel,
I know that you're here with me.
Here in the love and all is well.
Our love is setting me free.

Into my life comes your light
Shining right through me.
Share with me your angel sight.
Through your eyes I will see.

Just as we planned, you flew from God's Hand
Straight to our destiny.
Angel in flight I feel you right
Here inside of me.

Death has no hold on the life of my soul.
That's what you proved to me.
Our kinship is old, timeless and bold
Forever our family.

SONG BY ROBERT FREY

CHAPTER 2

The Risk to Love

"Come to the edge," he said.
They said, "We are afraid."
"Come to the edge," he said.
They came.
He pushed them...
and they flew.

GUILLAUME APOLLINAIRE

E VERY TIME I REACH THE PLACE of openness and love for my ex-wife, it seems like she does something that hurts me deeply. Isn't it better for me to stay closed to her than to continually open and be hurt?"

These words came from a man in the midst of one of our workshops. He was asking for help. We made room for him to sit in the center of the group so that he could receive everyone's love and support.

There, in the focal point of the group's energy, we asked this man to concentrate on his love for his ex-wife. He resisted at first, explaining that it felt more like a self-indulgence in pain rather than something constructive. We persisted, however, and before long he was crying. We then asked him to visualize his ex-wife and reach out his arms to embrace her. His arms came up slowly and hesitatingly for a brief moment, then a look of fear came across his face, and he brought his arms down suddenly.

"I can't," he stammered. "She's going to hurt me!"

"How," we asked?

He appeared to be reliving some distant memory as he spoke.

"She's got a dagger in her hands...she's going to stab me in my heart unless I protect myself."

The fear was mounting within him.

We gently coaxed him, "Get back to the feeling of love you have for this woman, and stay with that feeling as deeply as you can. Allow your heart to be so big, with so many spaces in it, that her dagger can easily slide in without even having to make a hole." We had him breathe deeply to facilitate this. We also directed the group to come gather around him and gently place their hands on him.

He cried deeply, then a smile suddenly broke out through his tears and he spoke, "I can't believe it! It doesn't hurt! The dagger is in my heart and it doesn't even hurt! I see now that the sharp point of pain can only hurt in a closed, constricted space. In the spaciousness of an open heart the knife no longer has power to hurt me. My ex-wife no longer looks wicked!"

He opened his eyes and looked around at the group with the innocence of a newborn baby. "I've always given women the power to hurt me," he proclaimed. "Now I know the power of an open heart."

Several of the women in the group came forward and hugged him. It was one of the most beautiful moments we had ever seen in a workshop.

That day, we all learned in a deeper way what it means to "risk to love." This man had to take a giant risk, a leap of complete faith into unknown and scary waters. The love and gentle touches of the others in the group helped, to be sure, but it was a leap he had to make by himself.

Somehow we've acquired the notion that loving should be without risk. It's OK that the lottery involves risk. It's OK that business decisions involve risk. It's very understandable that predicting the weather is risky. In fact, we can understand and accept the risk in everything...*except love.*

Yet loving involves the greatest risk of all. The risk to love is the risk to become vulnerable. Like the man in the workshop, we can only love if we risk being hurt. Hazrat Inayat Khan, the Sufi master, once told his closest mureeds (students), "You see this delicate glass." He held up a fine crystal glass. "Sometimes I feel that I am this glass, and my mureeds step on me and crush me to pieces. Yet I willingly and joyfully become that delicate glass again and again. That is love." Inayat Khan wasn't angry or blaming his students for being clumsy with his soul. He was communicating the ecstasy of vulnerability.

Vulnerability is our greatest protection, for it implies trusting in the ultimate goodness of creation and then allowing for whatever might come. We can't be vulnerable if we open ourselves only to certain kinds of energies and protect ourselves from others. We are not vulnerable if we only open to the sweetness of love, but not to the pain of love. Our greatest protection is unqualified and complete openness.

The risk to love is also the risk to feel pain. Gibran in *The Prophet* says it very well:

> For even as love crowns you so shall he crucify you.
> Even as he is for your growth so is he for your pruning.
> Even as he ascends to your height and caresses your
> tenderest branches that quiver in the sun,
> So shall he descend to your roots and shake them
> in their clinging to the earth.
>
> But if in your fear you would seek only
> love's peace and love's pleasure,
> Then it is better for you that you cover your nakedness
> and pass out of love's threshing-floor,
> Into the seasonless world
> where you shall laugh,
> but not all of your laughter,
> and weep,
> but not all of your tears.

When Joyce and I moved from Nashville to Los Angeles in 1970, our closest friend (and neighbor) was Leo Buscaglia. Leo loved us both, but he had a little bit of a problem with me. He confronted me once: "Barry, I wish you would share your pain with me as well as your love. Until you do, I feel like your love is not fully given."

I didn't understand what he meant. Why did I need to share my pain with Leo. What pain? I didn't even feel pain. And *that* was the problem! I didn't feel sadness either. I only felt anger if pushed very hard, which only Joyce could do. However, I was given the chance to learn quickly...

Just a year later, after I broke the sacred agreement of sexual monogamy, Joyce felt betrayed and she left. Part of the time she stayed with Leo and part of the time with a very close woman friend.

I learned all about pain in just a matter of days. My heart ached. I felt empty inside. My muscles felt as heavy as lead. It was an effort just to move my body. I felt grief, remorse, and sadness. I learned how to cry. It was growth at an amazing speed, but it was sheer torture at the time.

One day I could take it no longer so I walked the three houses over to Leo's and knocked on his door. I felt I was going crazy and needed to talk to someone. Leo opened his door and stepped outside with me. (Joyce was in the house, and she didn't want me to know she was staying there.) At first he was angry at what he perceived to be my betrayal of Joyce. Then he noticed the change in me. I was in pain and reaching out for help. I remember seeing the softness come into his eyes and how good it felt when he finally held me in his arms. Then he became happy and excited and starting yelling in his passionate way, "Barry, you're real! You're a human being! You're a real person now!" After two years, our friendship was now open to a deeper level of love.

Joe Miller, another vocal and beloved teacher, used to scream full volume with a beet-red face, "You can get more stinkin' from thinkin' than you can from drinkin', BUT TO FEEL IS FOR REAL!!"

Now I understood. Along with the feeling of pain were the tenderest and deepest longings I had ever felt. It was a great love welling up from the depths of my shattered heart. The Sufi masters talk about pain being the "first call of the heart," and how the greatest love emerges out of the "ruins of a broken heart." Through this experience of pain I was learning to feel all my feelings in a deeper way. And my love was deepening too.

A few years after these experiences in Los Angeles, we met Pearl and Jerry in Mt. Shasta. Jerry was one of the most humble men we had ever met. He quietly and contentedly loved and served Pearl and the many of us who came to see her. While large groups met in the living room with Pearl, Joyce and I often sat in the little back room with Jerry, bathing in his quiet and unpretentious joy.

It was Pearl who transmitted the oral tradition of the "I AM" teachings and introduced us to the great unseen beings who, with tireless devotion, guide our every step on this planet. We spent hour after hour delving together into the sacred mystery teachings of the universe. Mt. Shasta was a source of much inspiration to us, and we traveled there frequently. In those early days of study with Pearl, we would sit with her, work to clear our minds (which was a continual effort), and finally enter into the "radiation" of our Higher Selves, a truly blessed experience.

One particular day, however, Joyce and I were having a terrible time. We were not getting along with each other and consequently nothing seemed to be going right. We were scheduled to see Pearl that day, but figured that our dark, gloomy moods would block any possibility of a spiritual experience. We wanted to postpone our appointment but something inside said, "Go!" The thought of going to see Pearl in that condition was a real risk. What if we just sat there gloomily the whole time? What if Pearl judged us for having such a low consciousness? Of course we had to go.

"How are you both doing today?", Pearl asked with her bright smile and twinkling eyes. We both wished she could have somehow by-passed that question.

"We're not doing too well today," I shyly replied. We described a few of the events of the day and revealed our unhappiness to her. I'll never forget the cute way she rubbed her hands together and joyfully answered, "Good, now our work can really begin!"

Our vulnerability was the greatest gift we had thus far brought to our meetings. That day, it turned out to be a doorway through which we could more deeply feel the great presence of light. Until we could bring our human selves into our special space of communion with Pearl

---

and this light, there could only be a partial learning. When we could accept our human condition, the feelings of sadness, anger, selfishness and all the rest, as a necessary part of our whole experience on earth, we could enter into a more complete spirituality. Through vulnerability, we had taken the great risk of humbling ourselves. And through this humbleness we not only received the gift of a deeper awareness of love, but we gave Pearl a wonderful gift as well. We gave her the opportunity to help us and, by doing so, raised her to a higher level of consciousness.

Before leaving that day, we went into the back room to visit Jerry. Although he hadn't seen us, he felt that we needed a little extra help that day, so he was meditating and sending us love. Unless we pointedly asked, he might never have told us. In his quiet way, he was modeling the humility we were learning about in the living room.

Perhaps the greatest risk we can ever take in our lives is the risk to become intimate with *one* other person. More than sexual intimacy, I am referring to allowing ourselves to get truly close to one other person. Not just physical nakedness, but soul nakedness. It's easier to have many acquaintances than to have one true friend.

People have given us numerous reasons why not to be monogamous. We've been told that it's exclusive. It's excluding the rest of the world. We've been told it's boring, too routine...lacking excitement. We've been told it's making one person special, and no one is more special than anyone else. Some have even confided that it's like putting all your money into one single investment. If it didn't work you could lose everything. Perhaps you can relate with one or more of these reasons.

I'd like to suggest that fear of vulnerability, fear of being hurt, and therefore fear of real intimacy, is behind all these reasons.

Is being monogamous excluding others? It can be. It is possible for two people to isolate themselves from the rest of the world out of fear of other relationships. But this then is not a healthy relationship and there can't be much joy in it. For a relationship to remain healthy, it must breathe, giving and receiving love with the rest of the world. A healthy relationship is balanced by openness and accessibility to others.

Then what about sexual openness with others? There is a way to simply let sexual energy, which is the energy of creation, flow through your body and consciousness. This is a wonderful experience which allows you to feel attracted to everyone and everything. Although it is also a physical experience, it is not centered in the genitals, nor is there genital arousal. And there is no need to do anything about it. It doesn't need to be fulfilled by action. It is fulfilling enough to simply let this energy be and experience it.

However, it is very easy to fool ourselves into *thinking* we are experiencing this kind of pure, spiritual openness. In an attempt to not exclude others from our primary relationship, we often end up excluding our mate and causing deep pain and contraction in the very relationship we are trying to expand. Sexual affairs are very tricky business. Although we can easily rationalize our interest in relating deeply with other persons, we have a responsibility to be absolutely honest with ourselves *and* with our original partner.

We have seen too many couples try to "spiritualize" their sexual affairs, trying to rise above the deep gut-level feelings that come up, and doing this in the name of "growth" or "expanding their relationship." Although the following story is about a man having an affair, men are certainly not the only ones who open sexually to others. Although not as common, we have seen quite a few couples where the woman has had the affair.

Louis and Elaine, a couple with two small children, asked for help during a workshop. They shared with the group that they had been trying to work through an affair he had been having with another woman. While Louis sat looking somewhat depressed and withdrawn, Elaine described in great detail the valiant effort she had made to love Louis no matter what he did. She figured that if she could love him unconditionally, he would lose interest in the other woman. To ask him not to see this woman would be un-spiritual, a form of conditional loving.

So she set out on a campaign to accept what was happening. She reached out in friendship to this woman. She invited her to dinner. She even attempted to develop her own friendship with her. She hoped that if she could just love them both enough, the affair would pass over like some dark storm cloud. In her quiet moments, however, a sick feeling very deep inside threatened menacingly to overwhelm her.

Louis meanwhile felt more and more guilty, became more and more depressed, and to escape these feelings he spent more and more time with his woman friend. The whole situation seemed to be getting worse, and was complicated by the presence of the two children who were growing unhappy as well.

We brought Elaine and Louis into the center of the group and had them face each other. We asked Elaine to share with Louis all of her feelings about his affair. She became very uncomfortable and then agitated, as she spoke. "That sick feeling is coming up again," she began. "I don't know what to do with it."

She looked more and more uncomfortable. We suggested she share the feeling with Louis, who seemed to be coming more to life himself.

"There seems to be only one word that goes with the feeling," she continued. "And it's 'no'."

"Good," we said. "Say it."

"No," she softly spoke.

"I think you have more strength than that," Joyce said. "Try saying it louder."

It took several tries, and then the feelings erupted.

"NOOOOOO!!," she screamed. "I do *not* deserve to be treated like a doormat, to be trampled on and then ignored whenever you please. I am your wife. I am the mother of your children. I am a human being with feelings. I will *NOT* let you defile our family anymore."

In that moment, Elaine looked like a lioness defending her cubs. Then she collapsed in tears while Louis held her and stroked her head lovingly. When she finally lifted her head and looked into his eyes she saw that he had been crying as well. Louis looked at his wife as if for the first time and then tenderly spoke.

"I never knew you loved me that much!"

Elaine's "no" was the highest expression of love, for in that moment it was the deepest truth of her being. We learned later that this gave Louis the courage to end the affair. He desperately needed to know that Elaine loved him enough to take a firm stand in the situation. Her attempt at loving acceptance was a noble effort, but was not her deepest truth and therefore was interpreted as "wishy-washy" and indecisive by Louis. Elaine's risk to love was the risk to say no to a situation which was literally making her sick.

In our attempts to be more spiritual, we falsely believe that "yes" is a higher response than "no." Each is just as important as the other. In fact, if we are afraid of saying "no," then saying "yes" will have little power. The Islamic Zikr, a prayer of remembrance, is an illustration of the importance of saying "no." The Arabic words repeated, sung, or chanted by millions world-wide are: La Illaha il Allah. "La," the first word of this powerful zikr, means "no." The literal translation: "No, there is no God but God." More loosely: There is nothing else but God. All else is illusion in this world. The first word, "La," is like wielding the sword of truth, cutting through and negating all false pretenses. The powerful "no" clears the air for the affirmation that God is everything.

What we've discovered in our own relationship, through our own struggles, is that deep trust takes time to develop in a relationship, especially in the area of the sexual relationship. It is something which needs careful cultivating and nurturing. When you are in a committed relationship, when you have found a partner with whom you can go to God, and you allow yourself to *act* on sexual attractions outside the relationship, you are setting back this process of cultivating trust. It creates a wound that needs to be healed.

Of course there are two sides to every coin. "Sexual affairs" have brought tremendous growth and change to couples. Sometimes they have stayed together and healed the wound. Sometimes they have separated. But always they have grown.

I want to convey how it's been for Joyce and me in the seventeen years since committing to monogamy. After the healing of our wound, we have been deepening our trust ever since. Making love has become something very sacred and precious to us, a way of praying with our bodies. The physical love-making is less frequent than in our early years together, but the bonding is so much more present, the trust and joy so much sweeter. Because neither of us needs to have extramarital sexual experiences, we have been free to make our own sexual relationship the highest expression of our love and trust, and we feel that there's so much more...!

Let's look at the other reasons I mentioned for not being monogamous. Some people actually feel that it's boring to enter into a committed love relationship with just one other person. In our experience, whenever someone complains of "being" bored, it means they're boring themselves, and not taking responsibility for doing so. People get "bored" because they are wanting someone or something *else* to entertain them. If they're not willing to entertain themselves, no amount of external entertainment will really satisfy them.

Occasionally we will hear someone say, "One person can't meet all of my needs." I remember one man I saw in counseling who had two girlfriends. One was more earthy and stable. He went to be with her when he needed a quiet, calming time. The other was wild and exciting, which he felt helped him to "break free." It was fun and fulfilling for a while. He felt that the combination of the two women was meeting his needs better than either one could have individually. Then the problems came: the jealousy, the confusion, having to constantly choose between two women, and the lack of real depth and trust in either relationship.

The highest truth about "our needs" is that personalities (whether it's one or many) can never fulfill them. When we examine our different "needs" and ask ourselves, "What am I really needing?", we discover that our real need is for love, for spiritual sustenance. And this is available to us at all times. Love is ours for the asking, if we can open to it rather than expecting or demanding it from someone else.

Then we may feel that to be monogamous is to make one person special, and no one is more special than anyone else. It's true that no one is more special. Everyone has the same light within them. The commitment to enter into a soul-relationship with one person has nothing to do with making that person more special. As we said in *The Shared Heart*, "learning to love one other person completely, establishes in you a love for all humanity." It is easier, and less fulfilling, to love all of humanity in a general way than to love one person completely, including their weaknesses and habits. The closer we get to *one* other person, the clearer the mirror in which we see ourselves, and thus the more we are able to learn to love ourselves as well as our partner. Closely looking into a mirror is at times unpleasant, at times frightening, until we learn to love and accept what we see there. That kind of opportunity is especially made possible in the monogamous relationship.

Then there's the argument that monogamy is like putting all your money into one single investment. If it didn't work, you could lose everything. This is, of course, reflecting the very real fear of pain and loss.

Years ago, we had a friend who was recently divorced, involved in an unfulfilling relationship, and understandably cynical about relationships. She was also a sincere spiritual seeker, and could be very loving at times. Once, in a bad mood, she blurted out to Joyce, "You and Barry are too close to one another. Some day Barry will die and you'll be left all alone. Then where will you be."

Over the years, many people have said similar things to us, although not usually with the same vehemence as that friend. It wasn't until our spiritual odyssey took us to Chamonix in the French Alps in 1974, where we were to spend six weeks at a camp in an alpine meadow led by Pir Vilayat Khan, that a profound confirmation was to be given to us. It happened in the first few days of the retreat. In a meeting with Pir Vilayat, with his typical enthusiastic manner and expressive face he proclaimed, "You are one! Your work in this world is to live in that oneness! Spend as much time as possible together. Meditate together. Work together. Play together. Become a model for relationship for all to see!"

We felt that our relationship was blessed in that moment. Finally, after so many years, someone else could put into words what Joyce and I had intuitively known all along. It was *not* possible to be too close or to love each other too much. Immersing ourselves totally into love and complete sharing was our greatest insurance policy against the possible pain of losing one another. If one of us were to die, it would be the love that we have shared which would be of the most value in our grieving and healing process. In a way, our risking to totally love one another was only possible by risking total loss. Only by risking to lose one another was it possible to more deeply find one another.

CHAPTER 3

The River of Simplicity

Holy Earth Mother,
the trees and all nature are
witnesses of your thoughts and deeds.

WINNEBAGO INDIANS

INALLY THE BIG MOMENT HAD ARRIVED! We had looked forward to our first white water rafting trip all summer. People from all over the United States had come to join us for this six-day rafting workshop. Now as I sat at the campfire glancing at them, I began to feel nervous. I felt the weight of five-year-old Mira on my lap, and looked over at eleven-year old Rami. This was the first workshop that Barry and I had ever led in which our children were included as well. There was no special care arranged for them. What would it be like to lead our first totally outdoor workshop, care for the children and participate in the rafting experience...all at the same time? I knew I was capable of doing each one independently. But all three at once? I had my doubts.

Steve Bollock, our trusted friend for many years and river guide, sensed my resistance and gave me a reassuring hug. This trip had been his creation. He had sensed the beauty of combining our healing work with a river experience and had relentlessly urged us forward to this point. Behind my nervousness, doubt and fear was the calm, inner assurance that this experience would help me to grow in a wonderful, if perhaps unexpected way.

Before the greatest growth we often experience the greatest resistance. I heard the muffled roar of the Klamath River several yards beyond our campfire. Its steady flow with no resistance urged me to do the same. To my fear and doubt the river sang of the need to let go and surrender into the source of its power. "I will play with and care for your children," the river laughed. "Trust *me* to lead and heal this faithful group of participants," it urged as it gracefully danced around a boulder. "Have fun with me," the white water called.

Tomorrow this river would carry us all on an unknown adventure. Each of us was being asked to trust, to flow with the same surrender as did the river. None of us knew or could comprehend just how wonderfully nature was going to heal us.

My reverie was interrupted as our head river guide held up a black rubber bag. We had six guides for the trip. Each one was devoted to helping us all feel comfortable and well cared for. Their sense of service and love of nature was inspiring. "This is how to pack your black bag," David, our head guide, continued. We were told what to bring and what not to bring. All of our belongings needed to fit into this rather small bag. The girls and I had prepared for this part of the experience long ago. Each girl was bringing a small plastic bag with her very favorite toys in it. To go off for six days without toys was unthinkable. Each small toy had been *very* carefully selected.

The next morning we were scheduled to depart at ten. The group was all ready to depart except for Barry and our dear friend Charley Thweatt. Charley works with us on most of our longer workshops, adding his gift of healing music and song. At 10:45 Barry and Charley were still on the phone. If letting go and trusting that our children would be all right was hard for me, letting go and trusting that the rest of the world would be all right was hard for Barry and Charley. Finally a stern command from a river guide yanked them away from the outer world. So, saying good-bye to civilization, phone calls, computer programs, bank accounts, beauty salons, comfortable beds, time schedules, flush toilets, warm water and grocery stores, we took off down the river. Our group consisted of twenty-two participants: a dentist, a business man, two pregnant women, an engineer, a miller, a weaver, a poet, a medical doctor, a chimney sweep — a whole range of participants. Then there were six trained river guides, a thirteen-year-old trainee, Barry, Rami, Mira, Charley, me and our three-year-old golden retriever, Bokie. Although we were all from very different backgrounds, none of that mattered. The only things of true importance were our love, our desire to learn from nature, and our willingness to risk.

My insecurity must have been obvious in those first few minutes of the trip as I checked and double checked Mira for safety. During the first rapid, I held onto her so tightly that she complained, "I'm alright, Mama! Let's just have fun." As we approached the next rapid, Steve suggested it would be fun to get out and swim through it. Sensing my fright he added, "This trip is also about taking risks with your body, trusting your own strength and trusting the flow of the water. This rapid will carry you very quickly to that big boulder and, just when you think you will crash, the water will carry you to a quiet eddy (side pool). Keep your feet forward and don't resist." My heart urged me to try this new adventure but my mind panicked at the deafening roar of the large and awesome rapids ahead. "Don't be foolish. Stay in the boat," my doubting mind suggested. Just as my "reasoning" was beginning to win out, Steve shouted, "Jump in now if you want to swim this rapid. Remember, don't resist." "Go!" urged my heart, and in I jumped.

Seconds later, I felt my reasoning mind had been correct as the rapid carried me swiftly along, sometimes sweeping me under water with its force. Then I felt as though my fears were being totally confirmed as the turbulence carried me uncontrollably towards a huge boulder. Traveling at incredible speed, I felt sure I would end up in a wheelchair after my encounter with that boulder. At one point, when my head was above water, I saw Rami, Mira and Steve smiling at me from our boat. "They don't realize I am going to crash in a minute and it'll all be over," my thoughts raced.

Just when it looked as though the rapid was going to smash me into tiny bits on the rock, the water quickly carried me around to a quiet pool, just as Steve had said it would.

Standing in the quiet water waiting for our boat, I reflected on the last several minutes. I had been willing to take the risk to jump into the rapid, but the whole time I had resisted the decision in my mind. With surrender and trust, the whole experience would have been absolutely fantastic. How often are we guided to take a risk in life, our heart urging us to jump into the experience? We jump and then resist with our minds causing much struggle and unnecessary pain. As we learn to trust the voice of our heart, the rapids and rough places can actually be fun and exhilarating. The water, or lessons of life, may seem about to crush us on a big boulder or barrier. But, whether we hit this boulder or not, the question is: "Do we resist or do we flow with the river?" Eventually, we are carried around to a quiet pool of healing and reflection, giving us the strength to continue to flow down our river of life.

As Steve extended his hand to pull me back into the boat, he smiled and said, "Wasn't that wonderful!" His face expressed such confidence. Knowing the river as he did, I felt sure that he would never ask me to do anything that would be harmful. Sitting back in the boat I reflected on how God also knows the course of our lives so completely and would never guide us into situations that would be harmful. We are asked to trust our higher guides just as I had been asked to trust in my river guide.

The next morning, sitting in the sand in the shade of trees, the river flowing by, the sacredness of this wilderness area seemed to work its magic as barriers to loving were quickly seen and released. After three hours of opening our hearts to one another we were a bonded group singing together. Our group had become as one. From then on, each person became very sensitive to the healing needs of one another. We all dove into the water and played as children. Opening our hearts to one another in love also brought out our child-like natures.

The next day we were all going on a special hike to a waterfall and needed to leave early. Barry, Charley and I met with the group for meditation while the river guides made breakfast for us. We decided our theme for the meditation and the day would be our Heavenly Mother, the feminine principle of God. We decided to concentrate on feeling Her presence in our life for the entire day, and also to practice being instruments for Her love. Through sharing together, we realized that the female aspect of God is constantly loving us, seeing our beauty and strength and urging us forward to become all that we can be.

We decided to practice this concept by appreciating our river guides. We chose four people to give extra love and appreciation to each river guide. We decided it was best to do this in a casual way, without them suspecting our plan.

As our group slowly made its way over to the kitchen area, the guides were busily preparing french toast for the group, their faces showing their concentration. Barry and I remained up on the hill to watch the scene. A smile of amusement crossed our faces as we observed a woman going over to one of the guides who was busily cracking eggs. She spoke to him for just a moment and then gave him a hug. The man's face brightened as he resumed his task with greater joy. Then we noticed a man approach one of the women guides, speak to her softly and give her a warm and wonderful smile. She skipped back to her work. Within a half hour, each guide had been appreciated four different times. They were singing and joking as they flipped the french toast and there was an air of celebration and joy. Barry and I thrilled to see our loving group. Heartfelt appreciation is a powerful tool to help a group come together in peace and joy.

Soon we saw the river guides reaching out and appreciating members of the group. Appreciation is contagious. It fills both receiver and giver with happiness.

A short trip down the river brought us to the Ukanom Creek and our hike to the sacred twin falls. Matt, our big and gentle river guide, explained that this one-hour hike was difficult and would require us to push past our sense of limitation. He also explained that we would be rewarded with a view of a double water fall cascading into a large crystal-clear pool.

I glanced around at our group and saw a look of silent determination on each person's face. Some of these people had only hiked neat wooded paths and city streets. What a difference this was going to be! Then I glanced at little Mira and my heart began to pound. How did they expect Mira to make it? Lloyd, the river guide who was the most sensitive to Mira, came running over. "Barry and I can help Mira. It'll be fun," he offered with a smile. My mother's heart feared the rock ledges, cliffs and ice-cold pools. I was all set to suggest that Mira and I stay back when she joined hands with Lloyd and Barry and glanced back at me with eager excitement. Not only were we taking this treacherous hike, but we were also going to do it in silence. Each person was to anticipate the needs of the people close by. Strong hikers mixed with those of little experience. I stayed back so I could watch Lloyd,

Mira and Barry like a hawk.

We silently progressed up the river, over rocks and boulders, sliding along ledges and over cliffs. Occasionally, the only choice was to swim across the deep ice-cold pools. Mira smiled the whole time as Lloyd and Barry teamed with precision, guiding her along with their strength yet giving her the feeling of doing it all herself. Everyone was hiking very well over the dangerous sections except our dog Bokie who several times gave in to fear and had to be carried by Charley.

Walking in silence we became very aware of the beauty of this wilderness area and we all began to sense which rocks could carry our bodies' weight and which to leave alone. The entire walk proved to be a powerful meditation, bringing us a deeper awareness of the earth and our footsteps upon it. We felt the earth as safe and protective of our bodies, just as we had in the morning meditation on the Presence of the Mother God.

Just when we felt we couldn't walk another step, there was the double waterfall pouring into a deep pool! I eagerly dove in and swam. Barry dove in too and, with great effort, swam between the water falls and climbed up on a ledge behind them. I tried to join him but the force of the falling water kept pushing me back several feet from the ledge. Another man dove in, swam furiously, and finally reached the ledge. I tried again. When I was almost within arms reach of the ledge, the water's force again pushed me back. A few other women and men tried and were similarly pushed back. A few more of the strongest men in the group tried and after several attempts reached the ledge. Finally seven men sat on the ledge behind the falls. Like me, a dozen people had failed and were sunning themselves on the rocks.

I felt frustrated. Why couldn't I reach the goal of the ledge? Try as I would, I'd get to a certain point and be pushed back. Now I was in battle, trying to prove my strength as a woman. I called forth all of my strength, put my head in the water and swam. Just as my hand touched the rock, and for a split-second I thought I had made it, I felt the full impact of the falls upon my body. I was pushed under the water only to bob back up in the middle of the pool.

I looked carefully at the waterfalls and the seven men sitting behind it. A little voice spoke within my heart. "Does joy come only when we reach our goal? Or is joy to be found every step along the way as we attempt to reach the goal? Is the goal the ledge or is the goal to feel joy?" I felt my sense of competition with the men falling away and giving birth to the sheer thrill and satisfaction of trying. Each attempt I made after that left me with a feeling of exhilaration. It became an ecstatic feeling to be pushed back by the force of the water. The goal of the ledge was no longer important as I became immersed in the joy of trying.

How many times on our spiritual paths do we despair over our progress, and the goal of total awareness of God seems just too far away? Sometimes we even compete with our loved ones over who will reach the goal first. It is at these times that we need to stop ourselves and realize that the goal is not some distant time or place. It is the joy to be found in our everyday attempts.

The rest of the day we rafted down the river. By six p.m. we were a very tired group. After a short discussion it was decided we would camp at the next level spot. However, the next level spot proved to be less than ideal. The beach was muddy and the shallows were choked with weeds. Stepping out on land, we found bear droppings and large ants everywhere. The morale of our group was at its lowest point. We were tired and hungry and wanted to stop, yet this place wasn't right. Our guides worked to silently unpack the boats. They didn't like the spot either, but staying seemed like the practical thing to do. We had decided to spend the next morning at camp to continue the workshop part of the experience so we needed a good spot. Our group wandered around grumbling. Finally one of our pregnant women spoke out, "I just can't stay here. It's the wrong place for us!" Her remark became contagious and soon half the group wanted to leave. We felt there would be a place which would better nurture us. Many in the group were feeling that tomorrow would hold a very powerful experience for all of us. We needed the right environment. Our band of rebels prepared to meet the river guides who by this time had half the gear unloaded. "This isn't the right place!," we presented with as much diplomacy as we could muster. After some initial resistance because of all the unpacking that had been done, and the late hour, one of the guides spoke up, "There's another place about ten minutes down the river, but I'm not sure it's big enough for all of us. If it isn't, we would have another two hours journey ahead of us to the next level spot."

Every one groaned! The thought of rafting until eight or nine p.m. was not very pleasant. Half of us wanted to take the risk of journeying to the other spot, half wanted to stay. A full rebellion threatened to break out. I led a "R I S K" cheer, using my skill as a junior high school cheerleader. However, few were convinced. Our group was split down the middle. Then our tall businessman spoke, "I feel a power spot for us all down the river. I must take the risk and go there." We were silent for a moment. Each one of us pushed past fatigue and hunger and realized that we were all feeling the pull of this place of power.

In silence we helped repack the boats and began our journey down the river, realizing that we would either stop in ten minutes or go another two hours. Ten minutes later we beached the rafts and explored the new spot. After a few minutes we discovered a hillside shelf which would be perfect for the next day's workshop. Barry then looked to the left of this spot and saw a large Indian burial mound. Rocks were carefully placed forming a tall hill which over the years had been covered with moss and pine needles. We all felt the power of this very special spot. Sleep was wonderful that night.

The next morning I led a meditation on remembering, going back to the point before we were born when we each saw our life stretch before us and felt what we needed to learn and master. At the end of the meditation I noticed our tall businessman who had spoken up the evening before. His face was filled with grief. When he saw me looking at him he burst into tears. "I remember being in this spot before," he began. "I remember a life in which I was the chief of a small tribe that lived in this spot. I loved my people so much." His voice choked with emotion as he continued. "I was here the day many were massacred. I lived long enough to bury them in that mound. Then I died of a broken heart." As he spoke and cried, we all began to relive the experience with him. "When I received the notice of this rafting trip on the Klamath River," he continued, "I knew I had to come. In this life I've never been on this river, yet it has all seemed so familiar. I so deeply feel the pain of my lost tribe. They were all killed and their beautiful ways will never come back."

As he spoke his face held grief, despair and sorrow. He truly was the picture of a broken man, a chief who had died of a broken heart. Barry and I help people to recognize and experience pain in their lives.

However we do not encourage people to dwell in that pain. Instead, we urge them to move on. The pain can become as a friend, teacher or guide helping us to grow and learn. The object is not to dwell on the pain, but to learn from it and move on. This man was strikingly handsome and his manner was warm, friendly and loving. Despite his adventurous, happy nature, his eyes held a deep longing and sadness. Even when he laughed, his eyes held the sadness. Now he was using his inner eyes to see into the source of that pain. His grief was deepened by each member of his tribe that he remembered being killed.

We asked him to stand up before us and recognize himself again as the chief and the group his tribe. As he stood up he once again burst out crying at the image of how we would be killed. We asked him, knowing our fate as a tribe, to give us his last words of inspiration as our chief. He looked puzzled for a moment and then finally spoke, "I need a staff or stick to lean on." Ten "braves" immediately set out in pursuit of a stick. Within a few minutes ten assorted sticks lay at his feet. He examined them all and finally picked up a twisted old staff. "Yes, this is the one," he replied in satisfaction, and stood holding his staff upright.

"Remember to give us your last words of inspiration, and see your tribe living on in all of us," I urged.

We are usually not given full memory of past lives, as it is best for our spiritual growth to concentrate on our present life. It is more productive to stay in the here and now, rather than dwelling on the past. However, sometimes we are given a memory of a past life as a gift or tool in our growth process. As I wrote in the first chapter of this book, I was given the memory of Anjel as a daughter of mine in a previous life to realize the continuity of love and relationship. Knowing that she has never left me has helped me tremendously. Barry and I wanted this man to experience the continuity of the spirit of his tribe. We wanted to bring his attention to the ongoing spirit of his people, rather than dwelling upon the past life memory of how they were killed. We knew from our own experience with Anjel that, as he experienced the continuity of spirit rather than death and ending, he could begin to heal the grief and pain he had carried into this life.

Gradually, our businessman took on the appearance of an Indian chief, and he began to speak to us as if we were his tribe. The actual words that he spoke have slipped my mind. More important than his words, the feeling in his voice and his change of appearance are forever implanted in my memory. As he pushed past the memory of the massacre to the inspiration of Indian life, his whole manner changed. His eyes no longer held the sadness of seeing his tribe killed, but twinkled in wisdom and strength at feeling the glory of the Indian spirit. He realized that this glory still lived on. A tall man, he always seemed to stand slightly bent, as if his burden of pain was too much to bear. Now he stood in full stature, a picture of strength and noble qualities. Though he had died of a broken heart at the sad loss of his people, his wisdom, strength and ideals had never died. Pushing past the pain of that experience, he found a reservoir of strength and greatness that had never left him. We all felt changed and transformed in that moment. As this man was being healed of a long held sadness, we too were being healed and strengthened. In the light of the pain that he was letting go, our pain was seen and released as well. There is a beautiful saying from *A Course In Miracles*: "The holiest of all the spots on earth is where an ancient hatred has become a present love." This day we all witnessed this transformation, and the creation of a very holy place.

The sacred feeling of this experience lingered throughout the day as we traveled to Rocky Point, the site of an Indian village over one hundred years ago.

At sunrise the following morning we stood in a circle around a large campfire. The flat sandy area was perfectly suited for ceremony, so we began an ancient Indian dance. At the close of the dance we sat in silence around the fire while a soft drum-beat continued. Our theme in meditation for the day was the American Indian. We were guided to meet with our inner chief and receive his inspiration and blessing. Sitting with bare feet upon the sand, smelling the fire and feeling its warmth, listening to the flow of the river, and the sounds of the early morning birds blending with the drums, the visualization took on an added power.

At the end of the meditation, Charley sang a beautiful song about all of us being brothers and sisters in God's great family. I looked around at our group. Through our experiences of the last five days we had truly become as one family. Glancing at each person I saw a slight resemblance to the American Indian people. Though we were dressed in modern clothing with styled hair, each face held something of the wisdom of the Indian people. Living close to the land had made each one of us receptive to their Spirit. Jane and Paula, our two women river guides, spoke to us of the beauty of the Indian way upon this land. They also shared how a little over one hundred years ago there had been a total massacre of the Indian tribe at Rocky Point. They felt that our singing, dancing and invoking the Indian Spirit was helping to heal the land of the memory of that massacre.

The Indian Spirit had touched each one of us and had brought change, growth and healing. We had taken the risk to leave civilization for a few days and live simply upon the land. In this simplicity we had received the blessing and wisdom of the great tribes that lived before us.

Our civilization is relatively new to the land, compared to the ancient Indian culture which tenderly nurtured it. In our clumsy, aggressive way we took over the land and have allowed modern technology to rule over the Indian way of simplicity, honor and reverence for nature. But the blessing of the Indian wisdom is ours to receive every time we reach for simplicity and touch the earth. The greatness of our Indian heritage can live on in each one of us as we open to its influence. As we sit upon the land, we can be reminded of their reverence for all of nature. As we love and help our fellow human family, we can be reminded of the Indian's respect for each member of the tribe. As we choose moments for stillness and reflection, we are developing their skill of listening and inner knowing. As we take time to love an animal, we are reminded of their true communion with the animal kingdom. As we have faith in God's plan for our lives we are reminded of their total trust in the Great White Spirit for protection and guidance. The influence of the great Indian chiefs of our land can still be felt. It is a privilege to sit upon the land and receive the greatness of the heritage of our country.

When the last red man shall have perished...these shores will swarm with the invisible dead of my tribe. When your children's children think themselves alone in the field, the store, the shop, the highway, or in the silence of the pathless woods, they will not be alone...At night when the streets of your city are silent, and you think them deserted, they will throng with the returning hosts

---

that...still love this beautiful land. The white man will never be alone...Let him be just and deal kindly with my people, for the dead are not powerless. Dead, did I say? There is no death, only a change of worlds.

CHIEF SEATTLE

AT THE SIGNING OF PEACE TREATY IN 1853

The moment of sitting around the fire at Rocky Point was the highlight of the river trip for me. This was the moment in which I grew more fully into who I am, for in this moment I understood my connection to the American Indian. I could more fully understand my life and my attempts from early childhood to come back into a sense of simplicity and harmony with nature.

As Charley continued to sing and I sat gazing into the fire, memories and understanding filled my being. I saw myself as a small girl growing up in the city of Buffalo, New York. Our crowded city block had one vacant lot which was filled with old bent trees, weeds and dirt. As often as I could I sat in this lot and played. "This is the most wonderful spot of all," I thought, as my sense of wonder and strength were constantly renewed here. I often rushed from school, just so I could sit among the weeds and dirt and pretend that I was in the wilderness.

I thought of Barry and myself and our unusual writing method. Though we have a computer, neither of us chooses to use it when we write. Both of us can only write when we are outside, sitting in nature. We have tried sitting indoors to write, but it is unnatural to us. Sitting upon the earth, leaning against trees, and feeling the sun and the breezes, seems to activate our creative flow.

Our family is the happiest out of doors, so we go camping as much as possible. Nature seems to work miracles in us whenever we allow the quiet and the space for her healing magic.

Now I see the secret of the making of the best persons. It is to grow in the open air, and to eat and sleep with the earth.

WALT WHITMAN

IN *LEAVES OF GRASS*

After this powerful experience around the campfire, we hiked to the old village site. We all quickly sensed the dwelling spot of the Indian Chief and sat in a circle around it. Barry and I asked each member of the group to take what they learned on this trip and make a vow for their return home to their families and their jobs.

David Wikander, our head river guide and owner of the Turtle River Rafting Company, spoke up. "I chose to start this company because of my love of nature, the river and the joy I feel when I see others growing on the river. Then the demands of the business became so great that I started spending all my time in the office and I hardly ever saw the river. My vow is to return to the river and leave the office work for someone who enjoys that, and trust that the business will run smoothly without my constant attention." We all applauded! David is an excellent guide, and his skills were so appreciated on our trip. People smiled as he spoke, for his words touched a truth in all of us. How often do we forsake work which we love the most, in pursuit of greater material gain or business opportunity? Though all the vows were slightly different, as were all the occupations to which people were returning, there was a central theme which flowed through. Everyone wanted to bring more simplicity into their lives, taking more time to be with their families and to be outside in nature. Simplicity had played a part in transforming us, and we all wanted to continue the process.

The healing power of nature is to be found in any area of our country. I remember when I first moved to New York City. I was told that since the neighborhood was unsafe we would have to use underground tunnels to walk from the hospital to the nursing school dorm. I felt my spirit dying as each sunny day I had to walk in underground tunnels. The only "fresh air" I breathed came from my twenty-first floor open window. Several months later I lay in the hospital as a patient very close to death. When I recovered I walked out of the hospital into the sunshine. I knew something had to change if I were to survive my two years in New York City. I met friends similar to myself who, for safety, would walk with me to the various parks in the area. Finally I found a place along the Hudson River where I could go, not be bothered too much, and allow the grass and water to strengthen my spirit. In my two years of living in New York City I learned that the healing power of nature can be felt even in a busy and crowded city. Once I learned how to be restored by nature while living in the city, my time in New York became more enjoyable.

Nature can also work its magic in relationships and family problems. In 1972, Barry had an affair which threatened to dissolve our relationship completely. It was the hardest period of my life as I felt I could never trust Barry again. I was staying at a friend's home when Barry called and asked if we could spend a day together hiking in the mountains. I told him I doubted if I could enjoy doing anything with him, but he urged me to try. When he picked me up I felt very sad, defensive and closed. He looked over at me and spoke, "I know it's hard for you to be with me. I just thought that perhaps we could enjoy the mountains together once more."

He drove to our favorite trail outside of our Los Angeles home. We decided that rather than talking, processing and expressing anger we would walk in silence trying to be aware of our footsteps and the beauty of the trail. After a mile we came to a slippery spot. Barry reached out to help me across. I had not allowed him to touch me in several weeks. I held out my hand and the warmth of his hand felt good as he helped me across. We continued walking hand in hand.

After several more miles we were tired and lay down in the meadow grass for a nap in the sun. The anger and resentful thoughts seemed to have gradually slipped out of my mind with each footstep upon the earth. The energy that it took to be closed had become too much, so I opened to the beauty of the surroundings. As I woke from my nap Barry was tenderly looking at me. I once again saw my beloved and we hugged in joy.

My grief over the ending of our relationship gave way to hopes for a new and better relationship. Though it took two more years to fully heal the hurt and mistrust, that day in the warm spring sunlight had helped us to take a quantum leap on our path back to unity.

We invite each reader to take the risk of simplicity, to abandon civilization, cars, radios, telephones, calendars and watches for a day or two, or even for several hours, to return to nature. Allow yourself to enjoy the gifts of our mother earth, laying upon her ground, walking her paths, climbing her rocks and wading in her waters. There is wonder, magic and healing to be found out of doors. And as you touch the earth, be aware of the spirit of the Native Americans. Their highest vision for our land was one of harmony, unity, strength and greatness. Their influence and wisdom can still be felt for any who are willing to touch the earth and receive.

Boarding our rafts for the last time, our group sang out one of Charley's songs, "I love you, you love me, it feels so good to open our hearts." Our happy group had indeed received the blessing from nature's simplicity.

Here is calm so deep,
grasses cease waving...
wonderful how completely
everything in wild nature fits into us,
as if truly part and parent of us.

The sun shines
not on us, but in us.

The rivers flow
not past, but through us,
thrilling, tingling,
vibrating every fiber and cell
of the substance of our bodies,
making them glide and sing.

JOHN MUIR

CHAPTER 4

Kinship With Animals

I have a dream...

I see us learning to treat the animals who are, in the greater scheme of things, our younger brothers and sisters. I see us realizing they, too, are expressions, in their individual ways, of the universal life-force. I see us acting from the knowledge that it is the same God-Force that gives us all breath.

JOHN ROBBINS

IN *DIET FOR A NEW AMERICA*

HEN I WAS TWENTY-FIVE years old I had a job working with emotionally disturbed boys on a vast ranch in the mountains outside of Los Angeles. I had always lived in the city, and this was my first exposure to the country. I loved being in the mountains and exploring the wilderness with the boys. I loved the colorful peacocks that strutted outside of my office window, but mostly I loved going to the barnyard and visiting the animals. They had five horses which were available for the boys to ride. And there was Betsy the pig, Noisy the turkey, Big Ears the donkey and my favorite animal, Bertha the calf.

Each day I looked forward to taking the boys to the barnyard. No matter what bizarre behavior they were exhibiting, a trip to the barnyard almost always had a calming effect upon them. Upon seeing our arrival, Bertha would shyly approach us, waiting for her little treat of an apple. The boys would hug her, pet her soft head and then rush on to the horses. I stayed with Bertha, talking to her and looking into her beautiful big brown eyes.

Bertha became my friend as well as a helper to me. On days that

---

I was troubled over a work situation, Bertha's calm peaceful manner soothed me. On days that I was upset over a problem in my young marriage, Bertha's unwavering trust reminded me of unconditional love. On days when everything seemed to go wrong, Bertha's predictability was a great source of comfort. She always came for her apple treat and then allowed me to pet her. I could count on Bertha.

Through my relationship with Bertha I was learning about the sensitivity and peacefulness of cows for the first time. I was also learning about my relationship to the animal kingdom. I learned that animals are not things. They are living beings, as much a part of God's creation as I am. Having only known one other animal in my life, my childhood dog Nicky, Bertha was awakening in me a kinship to all animal life. Through our special friendship I grew to also appreciate Noisy the turkey, and even Betsy the ever-dirty farm pig. My time in the barnyard was often the most wonderful and enlightening part of each day.

One evening I stayed to have dinner with the boys. Usually we were served a rather simple, but tasty meal. Tonight, however, we were served an elaborate roast beef. Midway through the meal the cook came out to ask how we were enjoying the food. The boys were very enthusiastic. "I'm glad," smiled the cook. "Our menus seemed so plain lately that we killed Bertha today."

Silence overcame our little group. One by one we pushed our dinner plates away. One by one we left the table, absorbed in our own thoughts. I went outside and stood by a tree, feeling terrible inside. The fact that I had just been eating one of my dearest friends and teachers was completely repulsive to me. In that moment I realized that Bertha represented my kinship with all animals. Just as Bertha was my friend, so were all animals my friends. The life within her was as sacred as the life within me. She was shot in the head without any honor or respect for the beautiful creature that she was. She had been treated by her killer as a thing rather than as a living being. I saw that each time I ate meat, I was eating another Bertha, Noisy or Betsy. How could I ever eat another friend again?

That night I went home and told Barry the story of Bertha. I also told him I felt we should never eat meat again. Barry looked at me intently. I could tell he was weighing my words. In a few moments he announced that from now on we would be vegetarians.

To this day I am amazed at how quickly Barry responded to my plea. Neither of us had ever heard of tofu or brown rice, and we really didn't even enjoy vegetables that much. We had never seen a natural foods cookbook, nor did we know the first thing about food combining. We were basically just struggling to get Barry through medical school on our meager income of three hundred dollars a month. We ate mostly cheap hamburgers, chicken and hot dogs. We both held such a respect for animals, though, and knew we were now being asked to make this change.

When Joyce announced that we would become vegetarians, I knew I had to accompany her on this new adventure. Neither of us knew, however, what a big change this would be for us, nor how much of a risk it would be. When we started thinking about what we would eat, and even more about what we would have to give up, we became worried. When we saw the enormity of this change in life-style, and how much work it would entail, we were very tempted to change our minds. It would be so easy to keep on eating what everyone else ate, and pretend there was no connection between our love of animals and the slaughterhouses. It could be frighteningly easy to forget about Bertha, or to let our minds rationalize that meat-eating was appropriate or necessary. But it was already too late to change our minds. The feeling of identification with the whole animal kingdom was deeply imbedded in our hearts. There was no turning back.

The following day we had the opportunity to take a much-needed vacation. We traveled to a campground north of Los Angeles, right on the wild Pacific ocean. Remembering our vow to be vegetarians, we had stopped and bought salad supplies. This was the only food we were sure vegetarians ate.

We were happily preparing our salad when an extraordinary-looking young man slowly walked up to our Volkswagon camper. He was dressed in ordinary clothes, yet his eyes were shining. He looked at us for a moment, then at the salad and said, "I'm glad you've chosen to become vegetarians. This will bring you much happiness in your life." We smiled at him and he slowly walked on.

We suddenly realized that he knew of our vow to become vegetarians. "How did he know," we said out loud together. We jumped out of our camper to find him. He was gone! There was no humanly possible way for him to have vanished so quickly. Nothing like this had ever happened in our secure little worlds of student and nurse. We each gave some kind of rationalization to the other, yet we inwardly suspected that we had been visited by an angel in human disguise. Now I reflect on the perfect timing of that visit. His words totally removed any doubt we were having about our vegetarian diet.

Barry and I were quiet vegetarians. We never talked about our diet unless someone asked. Even then we said very little. This was our choice, and we just figured we wouldn't bother anyone else with our point of view. Whenever someone would ask why we never served meat at our retreats we would simply say, "We don't eat meat."

We would have continued to be quiet about our choice of diet except for an unusual dinner we had at our house. A boy of thirteen came to cook dinner for our family and, in exchange, we gave a donation for his youth ambassador trip to the Soviet Union. We decided he should also bring his parents.

His father, John Robbins, walked into our living room and handed us the book he had just written, *Diet For A New America*. "That's nice," I thought as I put the book down on my huge stack of unread books. I was happy with my diet and felt no need to read this book. Still I liked

Risk To Be Healed

the man very much and picked up the book the next day to be polite. I was unable to put it down! Reading it caused such pain in my heart and yet I read on. John had felt strongly guided to do extensive research and then publicly expose the way most animals are being treated by the meat industry. I read about calves that are taken from their mother at birth, forced into cages so small they can never lie down, and kept under blackened horrible conditions until they are killed for veal. I read about chicks that are inspected at the moment of birth and, if found to be male, are thrown into plastic bags with hundreds of other male chicks all struggling for life. They eventually die and are thrown away. I read about pigs that are crippled from being kept in tight cages where they can neither stand nor move. When asked about his crippled animals one owner replied, "We get money by the pound, not because of posture."

Most people never hear how the animals cry at the slaughterhouses. They are being treated as merchandise, rather than the beautiful creatures that they are.

I wept for a long time after reading as much of the book as I could. I knew I could never sit back again and be quiet about my choice of diet. I remembered Bertha and her tender brown eyes. She was a magnificent creature capable of responding to love and gentleness. Beginning with Bertha, and following through with our change in lifestyle and diet, we learned of our oneness with the entire animal kingdom. We learned to respect the inner as well as the outer beauty of animals. Through Bertha and her barnyard friends, we experienced the possibility of humans and animals sharing this earth in peace and respect. And our deepening respect for animals has brought about a deeper respect for all of life.

For our homeschool project, Rami and I had studied Chief Seattle of the northwest. He was a wonderful, majestic chief who had welcomed and helped the early white settlers. He had given them everything, expecting they would treat him and his tribe with the same respect. When he signed the treaty with the white people he discovered they had taken all the good lands for themselves and left his tribe with waste land. Chief Seattle was given the chance to ask for one thing in return. He could have asked for more blankets, horses, or food. He could have asked that the Indians sacred burial grounds be preserved. But this was his one simple request:

I will make one condition.
The white man must treat the beasts of this land
as his brothers.
For whatever happens to the beasts
soon happens to man.
All things are connected.

May we take a giant leap in life and choose to honor and respect our animal friends and feel our connectedness with all of life.

One thing we know:
Our God is the same.
This earth is precious to Him...
This we know:
All things are connected
Like the blood which unites one family.
All things are connected.
Whatever befalls the earth
Befalls the sons of earth.
Man did not weave the web of life.
He is merely a strand in it.
Whatever he does to the web,
He does to himself.

CHIEF SEATTLE

CHAPTER 5

The Clarity To Feel

LAY SOUND ASLEEP IN OUR TENT, while outside the stars shine brilliantly and the air is frosty cold. A moment later, I am awakened and the voice within urges me to get up, go to the camper where the girls are sleeping, and begin meditating. I feel the cold air and then the warmth of Barry's body in our snug sleeping bags. "No! I don't want to," I sleepily respond as I try to roll over and go back to sleep. Of course there is no use trying to sleep again and, after a while, I rather grudgingly get up and stumble through the night over to the camper. I make some hot tea and, while enjoying its warmth, I close my eyes to meditate. Before long I know why I have been awakened. I am about to receive another chapter idea for this book.

I had just finished writing the chapter about Anjel. It had taken me almost three weeks working every morning and evening to complete it. When I was done, I had felt I really didn't have anything else to add to the book. With Barry's additions, that one chapter felt like a complete book on the healing power of risk-taking.

"Your heart will give you more ideas," Barry had smiled at me. I waited with expectancy to hear the next idea. My inner voice responded very clearly, "Joyce, write a chapter on the risk to be free of drug addiction and drug use...especially marijuana."

Then began what I amusingly call my arguments with God. "No," I protested, "Barry and I already talked about a chapter like that and we decided against the idea. The use of marijuana is especially controversial. We might turn off some people," I concluded.

The reply was simple and straight to the point. "Do you want to avoid offending people or do you want to follow your heart?" Sometimes the inner voice has no tact in exposing the truth. Not to be outdone by that one, I went on to my last argument. We both felt that a chapter on marijuana use would come across sounding too "preachy" or condescending.

Again my heart spoke.

"It would only sound preachy or superior if you and Barry were not absolutely honest about your own marijuana experience."

As is always the case, my ego had lost the argument. I knew what I needed to do. Lying back again in our cozy tent, I wondered how we would be prepared to complete this task...

During the next year divine wisdom led us from city to city where, by some remarkable "coincidence", recovery groups were very active. In several of the workshops all but a few people were recovering from drugs, alcohol or other addictions. We heard many stories, became well acquainted with the various twelve step programs, and asked questions. We were surprised at the number of people we met who had been abusers of drugs or alcohol. We were most impressed at how these people were now using the experience of past drug abuse to help them on their life's journeys.

People were quite open about their drug use. It is common knowledge that a person who is regularly using drugs such as cocaine, heroine or alcohol needs help. Often this help comes in the form of a loving friend or family member confronting the person and assisting them to receive the necessary help. However, when a person is regularly using marijuana, this tends to be rationalized as being "OK." It is seldom seen as addiction or drug abuse.

Last year, in my little "argument" with God, I was asked to

honestly look within myself at my own drug use. I looked deeply into myself and was as honest as I could be. I found that this approach was what taught me the most...

It was springtime in 1969. Barry and I had only been married a few months. One Friday evening after a mind-cramming week of medical school studies, we smoked marijuana for the first time. We smoked just a little that night, but it was enough to turn my life around. The colors were so vivid and we laughed at just about everything. We had a close and beautiful time.

That experience, however, turned into a habit. Soon we were smoking every weekend. Being a shy person, I began to depend on the marijuana in social situations. The drug made me feel light and uninhibited.

Then we moved to Los Angeles where Barry completed his medical studies. In this large city every one of our friends used marijuana regularly. Many of them either grew their own or had sources of high quality "grass" from Mexico. It was never a problem to get the "good stuff".

The use of marijuana became a regular part of life, as much as having a cup of tea. Wherever we socialized with others, joints were passed around. Puffing on the joints, we all felt very liberated, free, open and expansive. Life was easy and fun...as long as we were high.

In between these "highs," however, life seemed like a drag. We increased our usage. Barry never smoked during school nor I while working, but as soon as we'd get home there was the temptation again. It was so easy to light up and forget the tensions of the day.

This pattern might have continued if it wasn't for our relationship with Jack Schwarz. We had moved to Portland, Oregon, where Barry was involved in his psychiatric residency program. Jack was teaching his classes in Portland. We went to every class and grew to deeply respect him. He had much experience and a deep understanding of spiritual and metaphysical matters. There was a small group of us that had gotten quite close to him. At the close of the classes we invited him to have dinner with our little group. He accepted, saying he would not eat dinner (he was fasting) but would come to enjoy our company.

There were five of us who busily prepared a simple dinner. We all admitted to feeling a little nervous about having Jack as our guest.

"Let's get 'high'," someone suggested and someone else ran for the marijuana. We laughed as we smoked. Each of us felt confident that now we were "socially secure" and that our greatest qualities would shine forth.

The door bell rang and we all ran to meet Jack. We were laughing and smiling as we opened the door. His ever-present smile suddenly gave way to a more stern expression as he studied each one of us. We thought he just needed a little cheering up, so we laughed and joked and really thought we were being absolutely adorable. He continued to stare with the same sober detached look.

Finally he spoke, "You have all been smoking marijuana."

"Why yes," we replied, "as someone handed him a joint. He refused.

Then he looked intently at us as he spoke what was in his heart, "If you could see what I can see right now in your auras, you would never even touch marijuana again!"

He continued, hoping his words would find an opening in the haze around us. "You think you are being light and happy, but your aura is reflecting quite the opposite. In your drugged state you don't realize the negativity of the energy you are putting out. Rather than the love and happiness you feel you are expressing, there is fear, anger and paranoia."

He left shortly after that, explaining that we were unpleasant to be with right then. We all thought *he* had just been in a bad mood himself, and we smoked even more, but each of us started thinking about his words.

I remembered that our closest friend at the time did not smoke. He had told us that he couldn't explain why but he didn't enjoy being with us when we smoked. He didn't feel tempted. It was simply unpleasant for him to be near us.

Barry and I began to experiment with not smoking in social situations. We went to parties where everyone smoked and we casually passed the joint along. Soon everyone would be laughing, but to us there *was* something unpleasant about their energy. We began to realize that what Jack had been trying to tell us was true. Our days of smoking marijuana were drawing to a close.

Fortunately the quitting was very easy for us. At the same time that we saw the need to quit, we were opened more deeply to the spiritual path. The energy that had once been invested in getting "high" was now turned towards meditation and inner growth.

Three years later I was pregnant with Rami when a friend came to visit us. I had a very high respect for this man. We were finishing dinner when he pulled out a joint and lit it.

"What are you doing!," was our shocked reply.

"Marijuana is a valuable tool for experiencing God," our friend casually replied. "It works better than meditation."

Now this was a new twist. What he was saying made a lot of sense to us...because we *wanted* it to be true. There was a part of us that missed getting "high". It was so easy and fast, while the meditation and yoga route we were following seemed quite slow. Then we pondered, "If we used the marijuana as a sacrament, if we made it a spiritual experience, our "high" would be pure." We prayed over the joint, blessed it and lit it.

Ah! An easy way to enlightenment.

Just smelling the smoke in the air, unborn Rami inside let me clearly know that she would have no part of this drug in her body. I couldn't smoke, but I continued to observe Barry. At first there was a beautiful lightness about him and he was exclaiming, "Oh, God is so beautiful!" Then a very subtle change came over him and I did not feel comfortable being around his energy. The next day he seemed distant and we didn't get along very well.

When we used marijuana to get "high", to forget our problems and move into what we thought was a more exciting space, it was easier to stop than when we were tempted to use it to enhance our spiritual growth. This was much harder. In my pregnant condition, I was spared the temptation to smoke and this continued throughout the two years that I nursed Rami. For Barry, and I think for many who are seeking God, using marijuana and other drugs such as "ecstacy" or LSD for spiritual reasons becomes a very big temptation. There are times when we all feel far away from love, and we are tempted to take something to alleviate this feeling.

We began to realize that many of our friends on the spiritual path were smoking quite regularly. We also learned of new age teachers who were using marijuana to enhance their talks. In my maternal state I sat back and watched. There did seem to be an opening in people when they first smoked. They did seem to be experiencing a higher state of consciousness. But then something seemed to get cut off. I would feel as if I were left hanging, waiting for them to express the God energy that I knew was possible from them. Whenever I would mention this observation, these people would deny it very strongly. Marijuana, I feel, is one of the most strongly defended drugs, perhaps especially among those who use it for "spiritual" reasons.

Barry smoked from time to time. The distance between us after he would smoke became more and more obvious. Finally I asked him to stop altogether and he did. He obviously wasn't very attached. We enjoyed our little baby Rami and for the most part never thought about smoking. Every once in a while I'd notice Barry's little "stash" in the cupboard. I knew he wasn't smoking anymore so I asked him why he didn't throw it away. "Oh you never know," was his far off reply. I noticed I didn't make any attempt to throw it away either.

Throughout Rami's babyhood and until she was four and quit taking her long afternoon nap, I meditated from four to six hours every day. This intense spiritual practice contributed to my becoming very sensitive to subtle changes in energy. Shortly before this period ended for me (two children and a much busier life brought my meditation practice to more like a half hour a day), my parents watched Rami so Barry and I could go on a small backpacking trip. We were thrilled to be alone again for the first time in four years. The rugged Big Sur coastline made an inviting place to camp and be alone.

Sitting around our first campfire, Barry pulled out a little bag. A friend had given him marijuana that he had grown himself with the utmost care. He told Barry that just one puff was all that was needed to "feel one with God." Oh how enticing these words were. "One with God," I repeated slowly. Temptation lurked as I mulled the words over in my mind. Previously we had taken drugs to get "high", to forget our problems or to get closer to one another. In this beautiful spot on the ocean we already felt naturally high and we felt very close to one another. Still...*one with God*...such an enticing experience! We could always get a little higher than we were feeling. We looked at each other and remembered with nostalgia the first time we smoked together.

"Well, let's try once more!," we both said almost in unison.

We decided to wait until after we had meditated the next day. With pure minds, pure hearts, and pure marijuana we felt we were bound to have a pure experience. We meditated in the morning in preparation for a holy event. I hadn't smoked in seven years. It had been about four for Barry. Each of us were very different than when we were smoking regularly. We prayed and kissed each other. We asked God to use the experience to strengthen us spiritually. We *were* strengthened, but not in the ways we had anticipated.

Finally, we smoked. At first the colors of the ocean radiantly glowed. I felt myself expanding and opening. I knew this experience as the beginning of deep meditation. I was just about to sit back and enjoy the ride, when suddenly I felt as if a door were closed. I knew the ride of expansion was much longer and more beautiful.

"This is as far as you can go with the drug," my inner voice calmly replied, "Now you have to experience the drug and its effects on your body."

I felt the drug-induced speediness and agitation and helplessly watched as my once peaceful mind became filled with thoughts. The thoughts in themselves seemed harmless, but my mind would uncontrollably jump from thought to thought. I looked over at Barry and he confirmed that he was having similar experiences.

Years before, when we had taken the drug, we had enjoyed the ride to the door, not even minding that the door had been closed. We hadn't known any difference. Now we knew what lay beyond that door, a realm of God consciousness that could only be reached without drugs, a realm that lasts day to day, strengthening and bringing us wholeness.

In addition to how my mind jumped from thought to thought, I was aware of other energy changes. I remembered Jack's words to us about the unconscious negative changes in our auras. In my beginning years of marijuana use these changes were hardly noticed. Now with much sharper sensitivity I was very aware. "That's why it's unpleasant to be around someone who is smoking when you're not," I thought.

The day passed very slowly. It had only taken one instant to smoke the drug, but laborious hours for its effects to wear off.

The next morning was not easy. Even though it had been twenty four hours since we had smoked, the skies of our beings were still fogged over. The only clarity I received in my meditation was the need to take a firm stand about drugs. I told Barry and we both pondered this for some time. Each of us knew in our hearts what that stand was. We also knew what a big step it was for us. It was our "risk to be healed" of all drug addiction. We knew we had to vow to never smoke marijuana again and to loosen ourselves from the last bit of temptation. As long as we weren't smoking but kept a secret "stash" in the cupboard just in case, we hadn't truly stopped.

Towards the end of the day we were ready to take the big step. We sat in front of our campfire and vowed to never use marijuana again. We ceremoniously offered the little packet of drug to the flames and then, as a final act of sincerity, Barry threw into the fire the pipe we had always used and had kept *for sentimental reasons.*

That was eight years ago. We are now free from drugs. This freedom is a most wonderful feeling. We both now know that there is no material substance that will help us feel God. All that we need to feel joy, light and oneness is within us.

In the town of Medjugorge, Yugoslavia, Mother Mary has been appearing to a small group of children for several years. The children enter a beautiful state of ecstasy throughout these visions. Mary wanted to reveal the greatest sorrows in her heart to one particular girl. She showed the girl a vision of children dying of hunger in Africa. Then she showed her violence in Asia. Finally she showed her young people in America using drugs. Through this vision, she was asking for the people of the earth to help in these situations. Children are desperately needing strong role models of how to live in the world and still be happy without drugs (including alcohol). How can we be models of love, inner strength and self-disicipline for our own children when we secretly have our own drug habits?

Several years ago, while leading a workshop in Hawaii, I was drawn to one man in particular. He was a shy man who sat back and watched, but now he was wanting to speak. He explained to our group that he had seemed to fail continually in life. His marriage failed. He had a hard time staying interested in a job. There were many things he wanted to do, but never quite got around to doing them.

Barry interrupted this man and pointedly asked about drugs. He reluctantly admitted to having smoked marijuana every day of his life for twenty years since he was thirteen. He also said it was the best thing in his life.

As he spoke those words, something very unusual happened to me. I began to feel as if I were being lifted out of my body and entering the great heart of the Mother God. I had never had this experience before. While looking at this man, I felt tremendous pain and started to cry very deeply. People wondered what had happened. All I could feel was that the marijuana was blocking this man's ability to fulfill his unique and wonderful destiny...to be a true servant of God. Because of his heightened sensitivity, and parents who perhaps could not understand it, he had taken to drugs at an early age to cope with the harshness of the world as he perceived it — and he had kept on every day for twenty years.

Still crying, I stroked this man's head with love and tenderness. For a brief moment in time I felt like a mother holding her precious child, knowing of his special mission upon the earth, and seeing him blinded to it because of prolonged marijuana use. I saw the miracles that could take place in this man's life if he just allowed his body to be completely free of drugs.

The man looked at me through the tears in his eyes and finally found his voice, "No one has ever cared *that much* about me." Along with the sadness in his expression, there was a hint of wonder and hope.

Our friend Robin in Tucson tells of working with recovery groups in prison. She herself is recovering from drug abuse. Even though drugs are usually quite easy to obtain in prison, she tells of numerous prisoners who remain completely drug-free. They speak about the wonderful sense of freedom they feel in their lives, an inner freedom they never knew outside of prison. Robin shared with us how much more imprisoned she had felt by her own drug abuse than these people who, despite their bodily imprisonment, were learning about true freedom by giving up drugs.

Our greatest hope is that all of us may know this inner freedom, and realize that there is no drug or substance that can bring the fulfillment we desire. Joy and happiness are our birth right. All we need to do is open our hearts and find it inside ourselves.

It was the middle of a weekend men's retreat. Steve, a man in his late twenties, was asking the group for help. He shared that his wife had left him after a short and very stormy marriage. We could all see the man's sadness although it was evident that he wasn't quite in touch with his feelings. The men moved closer to him in a gesture of love and support.

I asked Steve to share why the separation took place. He looked blankly at me and said, "I don't know." Then I asked, "What was your wife's reason for leaving you?"

"Well, she said it was because of my smoking marijuana." Then he quickly added, "But I've always smoked, and it's never been a problem for me."

I could see he was really convinced of this. "How much do you smoke?" I asked next.

"I only smoke one or two joints a day, just in the evenings."

"Uh oh," I thought, "he's pretty well defended."

"And how long have you been smoking?" I asked.

"Ummm, I can't remember. Maybe since I was thirteen or fourteen."

I paused a moment to reflect on Steve's answers. Here was someone whose whole adolescence and young adulthood was experienced partly through the haze of marijuana smoke. These are such powerful formative years, a time when a boy establishes his identity as a man, a time of rapid growth and change, and so also a time of confusion. As a friend who used marijuana only briefly once told me, "Life is challenging enough to absorb and understand even without the addition of an external factor (drugs) to confuse things even more!"

Looking at Steve, it was obvious to me that his marijuana habit was a major problem. I told him this, then added, "There may be deeper issues, but until you stop smoking, you'll have a very hard time uncovering them."

Immediately, another man in the group spoke up, "I smoke marijuana every day and I don't feel it prevents me from working on my deeper issues." Someone else confronted him, "Perhaps it's because you're blind to them."

I watched as the group of men were starting to become polarized. A whole intellectual debate was brewing. If we were to have a healing presence in the room, I needed to act quickly. Since the marijuana issue seemed to involve the whole group, maybe there was a way to include everyone in the process.

So without having a clear idea where it would lead, I asked for those men who smoked every day — or even almost every day — to sit in the center of the room. Steve and the other man who admitted to this kind of marijuana use immediately moved to the center. A tension mounted in the group of twenty eight men as one and then two others hesitatingly joined them.

"Good," I said as I instructed them to form a small circle together. "Now let's have those who use marijuana at least twice a week." Four more men gradually came forward to form a second circle. I looked at the men who were left and encouraged them, "This is the time to be absolutely honest with yourself. We're not here this weekend to judge one another. We're here to give support and especially to learn from each other." Two more men smiled nervously and joined the second circle. I thanked them.

"Now, how about weekly smokers?" One by one, a total of nine men finally sat together, forming a third circle.

"Great, now let's have the occasional users, anything less than once a week." Four men came forward, not enough to form a circle, so I asked them to sit outside the third circle.

There were five men left and myself, ranging from six months of abstinence to many years. One man had never smoked marijuana. We knelt around the perimeter of the concentric circles.

I didn't have the faintest idea of what to do next, but I felt it was somehow important to make a graphic picture of the whole group's marijuana use. For many in the group, it was a risk to publicly admit to using the substance. I confessed, "I really don't know what will come of this, but I feel if we can now share a little more from our hearts, we'll be able to learn a lot."

One by one, the men took risks by sharing their feelings about their use of marijuana. It was all very helpful, yet I noticed that the men speaking were always the ones who were more used to speaking in group situations. I finally broke in, "I'd like to hear from someone now who would ordinarily sit back and let everyone else do the talking. Now's your chance. We need your wisdom, too."

There was a moment of silence, and then one of the five non-users raised his hand. "I feel I need to share," he began in a quavering voice. "From the moment Steve began talking, I have been shaking inside, knowing I needed to share my story." He described a more than twenty-year marijuana habit, which he also had begun as a teen-ager. He choked up with tears as he related his difficulties with relationships, including the painful loss of a marriage and two children he adored. He described even cutting his habit down to weekly use, without any real noticeable change. Finally he concluded, "It has now been one year since I have used marijuana in any form. In this year, I have learned how to feel again. It has been the most precious gift of my life. I feel love. I feel pain. I feel loss, anger, sadness, joy. It doesn't matter to me what I feel. It is a blessing merely to feel again. In all my years of smoking, I didn't even know what I was missing. It took six months of abstinence before my feelings started to wake up, gently at first like tiny seedlings popping out of the ground after a very long winter."

A muffled sobbing from the center of the circle drew everyone's attention. It was Steve. The three other men in his circle were holding him with gentle fathering arms. His hands covered his face in a futile attempt to hide his shame. A respectful silence gave him permission to release many years of stored-up tears, and an atmosphere of reverence and nurturing gave permission for a boy to become a man.

Steve cried for quite some time before he was ready to remove his hands. He looked at the three others in his inner circle. Their eyes were also moist with tears. He looked at the second, then the third circle, and finally at those of us on the periphery. He saw a complete lack of judgment in that group of men. He felt the love and acceptance being offered to him. He sat up straighter and spoke, "I know what I have to do, and it's not going to be easy, but with the love and support I feel in this group, I know I can give up marijuana."

"Go ahead," I said enthusiastically, "make a vow."

Steve paused a moment, closing his eyes. "I vow to quit using marijuana or any other drug. I vow to feel again!"

One of the biggest smiles I have ever seen broke out over his face like a glorious sunrise. He was instantly smothered by the joyous arms of the men nearest him, while smiles filled the rest of the room. Other vows soon followed.

I personally feel Steve will win this battle, even though I haven't heard from him since that weekend. I feel this way because I saw a man wanting to feel, already tasting the fruits of his ultimate victory over his marijuana habit. I also know it won't be easy, especially as he delves more deeply into the pain he has caused himself and others. The temptation to run from that pain will never be more than one joint away. But feeling the pain will bring for Steve the healing of that pain.

The risk to give up marijuana (and all drugs) is the risk to feel. As we give up drugs, it is as if a fog covering our being begins to evaporate. We begin to see and feel more clearly, including those unresolved issues we have buried deeply within our souls. Yes, this renewed clarity can be painful at first, but it is a risk we must all take if we desire healing and true freedom. With willingness and perseverance, we will heal whatever it is that keeps us from feeling pure joy. Without the fog of drug use, we will learn to feel as never before, and we will reclaim our original freedom to dance in the light of clear awareness.

Man cannot discover new oceans
until he has courage to lose sight of the shore.

ANONYMOUS

CHAPTER 6

From Vocation To Vacation

*The secret of success is making your
vocation your vacation.*

MARK TWAIN

HIGHLY INTUITIVE FRIEND and guide on our journey once
told me my "vocation would someday become my
vacation and my vacation would become my vocation." It was 1972, and I was a resident in psychiatry at the University of Oregon Medical
Center in Portland. Even though I enjoyed many aspects of my work
and training, especially those heart-to-heart healing connections with
patients and staff, the work weeks of sometimes seventy hours and the
pressure to conform to medical psychiatry took a toll on my mind and
body. Time out for hiking and camping in the magnificense of the
Northwest became crucial for my sanity. When would this friend's
prophecy come true, I wondered?

Leaving the academic world of psychiatry, Joyce and I essentially
"dropped out" and used what little money we had saved to embark on
an adventure of spiritual seeking and study. Eventually arriving in
Santa Cruz, California, we found a place to live far from everyone. We
did hours of spiritual practices each day and saw just enough clients in
psychotherapy to support ourselves financially.

Psychotherapy has always been an interesting challenge for both of us. Although we enjoy it and often have a powerful impact on the lives of those coming to see us, we have never enjoyed seeing people all day long as other therapists do. In those early days we felt we were not strong or developed enough and therefore absorbed all kinds of energies from our clients. Our sensitivity was not yet balanced by the power of detachment.

Then, in 1976, along came Rami and we grew even more sensitive and inward — partly due to the influence of her presence in our lives. Our counseling clients became few and far between. There was a part of us that was relieved and another part that was concerned about our dwindling finances.

Once, during a visit with Baba Hari Dass, an East Indian Yogi who has not spoken for many years, we explained our predicament. He asked me (via his chalkboard), "Why are you not doctoring?"

I tried to explain, "I'm no longer interested in medicine. I'm more interested in meditation and studying consciousness."

I remember his knowing smile as he wrote on his chalkboard, "You have the personality of a doctor. Work in a hospital." He was known for his disarming bluntness.

I laughed at the preposterous image of me doing general medicine in a hospital — the white coat, the stethoscope dangling from my neck. I remembered my last year of training in medicine, and how sad I felt about what I perceived to be a gap between what I was being taught and real healing. I remembered choosing psychiatry with the hope that I would be working more closely with the deeper cause of illness rather than simply treating the physical manifestations.

Returning home after our visit with "Babaji", we had the sobering thought that perhaps I *was* running away from medicine. Perhaps I did have more to learn about treating physical illness. I thought of the story of the man who wanted to renounce money when he had never earned money in his life. His teacher sent him out to learn about earning money. He eventually became a wealthy man, accumulating all the possessions that came with wealth. Then, in a moment of *real* mastery, he gave everything away so that he could follow his original heart's desire.

Was I renouncing medicine prematurely...renouncing a lesson I

had not yet learned? Again I imagined myself working in a hospital.
This time it was *fear* that gripped me. And I knew I had to do it...

> *Do the thing and you will have the power.*

RALPH WALDO EMERSON

As I turned onto Kiely Boulevard in Santa Clara, Kaiser-Perma-
nente Medical Center loomed threateningly ahead. Here I was in the
city of Santa Clara, named after Saint Clare, the woman who risked
leaving the comforts of her home and family to follow Saint Francis in
a life of poverty...a woman who also spent a great part of her life *healing
the sick.* "Well," I thought, "working at Kaiser might not be a life of
poverty, but it might teach me something about healing the sick..."

The parking lot was enormous, with the only available parking at
its outer limits. It gave me that much more time to experience my
nervousness during the seemingly endless walk to the entrance.
Though I had only been away from medicine a few years, it seemed like
an eternity because of how much my life had changed in the interim.

I pushed open the large, heavy glass door and entered a strange
world. I'll never forget my feeling of being on an alien planet. People
rushing here and there, doctors being paged on the loud speakers, the
prominent antiseptic smells...I felt like turning around and walking
right back out that big door!

Somehow I made it to the fourth floor medical clinic where the
head nurse oriented me. She showed me a tiny cubicle of an office and
told me I would have a few minutes while my first patients were put in
my exam rooms.

I closed the door. I was alone at last. What was I doing in this
strange place? There were piles of medical books and journals on
shelves, on the desk, even on the floor...so much information to relearn
after my years away from all this, so much new information, a whole
new level of technology in only a few years. My mind started to spin
with the thoughts of all the study I needed, but then I thought of the
patients being prepared in my exam rooms. These were real people

with fears and joys and pains...people with feelings. "Dear God, help me to be effective as a healer. Use me as an instrument of Thy peace..."

A knock on the door jarred me from my prayer, and then a voice came from the hall: "Your patients are ready, Dr. Vissell." My patients were ready, but was I? What if my first patient had some obscure disease that I had barely heard about in medical school? Or worse, what if someone had something truly serious, like the early signs of a life-threatening illness? Would I know what to do? The fear and anxiety started rising within me...then I remembered the prayer I just uttered . I realized that these patients were being guided to me for a special reason. There was something I had to offer that they needed—every one of them. Maybe it wasn't my left-brain analysis of their symptoms, the *diagnosis* — that magic medical word that could put a box around their whole world, perhaps giving them the illusion that someone knew exactly what was happening inside of them. No...I had more to offer. I could love each patient as a child of God. In the guise of a physical exam, I could inwardly ask God's blessing upon the afflicted areas of their body and allow that flow of healing light to pass through my hands. Yes...and even more. I could learn from these patients, for weren't they also guided to me to teach me something — about myself, about healing?

Bolstered by this awareness, I opened my office door and stepped out into the giant hallway. I had a momentary thought that all eyes would be on me, the *new doctor*. But a reality-check proved otherwise. The doctors, nurses and clinic assistants were all too busy to notice what I was doing.

I approached my first exam room. There was a chart on the door. I lifted it from the rack and looked at it. A forty-eight year old man was complaining of a sore throat — not that he was actually complaining; this was medical jargon for his presenting symptom. Knowing only this, I knocked and entered the exam room. Inside, a tense, balding and slightly overweight man was sitting on the edge of the examining table. I greeted him with his name and smiled, reaching out to shake his hand. He took my hand but remained reserved without smiling. I noticed a suit and tie hanging on the clothes hooks. I was momentarily aware of my own untrimmed beard, my hair which was longer than that of any other doctor in that hospital (although pulled back neatly in a ponytail), and my hiking boots.

My patient, however, didn't seem to notice my appearance. It always amazed me how the white coat and hospital environment seemed to break down traditional cultural barriers. To this conservative-looking businessman I was simply "Dr. Vissell."

He told me about his throat pain and his unsuccessful attempts to relieve it, but his real concern was the frequency of his sore throats. Written all over his face was "cancer-phobia," and along with the fear of cancer was depression. I started asking the medical questions I had been taught to ask. Yes, he smoked and needed his "cocktails" before dinner to help him unwind from the pressures of his day at the office. I looked at his throat. It didn't appear serious. I felt for lymph nodes. There were none, but I inwardly asked that my hands be used as instruments of blessing, of healing. Somehow, the white coat made it OK for an unorthodox-looking man to gently touch and bless a very orthodox-looking man without arousing even the slightest discomfort or uneasiness.

The exam and "medical" part done, his symptoms explained, I was now free to gently probe deeper. It helped him to learn that the smoking was very related to the frequent sore throats, but I could see he had perhaps never experienced a doctor who was so willing to listen to him. I asked about his job, his relationships, his feelings about himself. I asked not as an "examiner," but as a brother or friend. Because of this, he was surprised by his own openness. There in that sterile little exam room a deeper communion was taking place, the doctor-patient roles were being dropped, and a healing atmosphere was being created. He left the room extremely grateful and uplifted. I left knowing so much more about real healing.

But there was a problem. I had spent forty-five minutes with my first patient, who was scheduled for a fifteen minute appointment. I was to later learn that these "minor" complaints took the other doctors no more than five minutes of patient-time, which allowed them to relax or read journals in their offices for ten minutes. The clinic assistant told me I now had two patients in the waiting room and one in my second exam room.

This harsh reality was to be my constant companion for the seven or so years I worked part-time at Kaiser. Sometimes it was almost too much for me. Occasionally there was someone who had serious medical problems. Once I spent over an hour with someone in a major life crisis. I ended up seven patients behind, with frustrated staff trying to hurry me and frustrated patients whose problems seemed to escalate because of the long waits. Sometimes I succumbed to the pressure. My heart closed, and I was "Doctor Machine," processing patients on the medical assembly line.

The chief of medicine was torn. He was sympathetic to my "humanitarian" approach but was also caught in the economics of big-business medicine. He was forced to tell me that I had to speed my pace.

I found I couldn't keep my heart open rushing between exam rooms. Once, I was aware of being behind, and an ulcer patient came in "simply" to have his prescription refilled. I saw a person caught in a stressful, anxiety-filled life, maybe even reaching out for help. When I found myself quickly writing out a prescription for some pills that would cut down on the acid-production in his stomach, causing who-knows-what somewhere else in his body, I knew then it was time for me to leave.

I finally quit. But I wasn't done with medicine. Next, I worked for the local county health department, which gave me a different view of the medical profession. While the Kaiser patients were largely middle class, the county patients were predominantly lower class. I worked half-time, twenty hours a week, which I perceived to be the upper limit of my involvement in the medical world. I worked with the poor, with drug addicts and with alcoholics. One morning each week I saw the prisoners at the county jail. While treating these patients, I was treated to an inside view of raw human struggle and desperation.

Some part of me felt very much at home with these poorest of the poor. It was the "Mother Teresa of Calcutta" part of me listening to Jesus' words, "How you treat the least of these my brothers and sisters is how you treat me." He was urging us to see God's Presence in all beings, no matter how sick, ugly, dirty or deformed. He deliberately sought out those who were unloved by others and gave them his time and blessing. His disciples were often the rejects of society, those who had nowhere to turn but to God and so were ripe for spiritual awakening.

Joyce, too, shared these feelings. While I was in medical school in

Nashville, Tennessee, Joyce worked for two years as a public health nurse. In 1968, there were many, especially Blacks, who lived in extreme poverty. Joyce visited and grew to love these people. Some of them had such faith in God and profound wisdom that she felt she was visiting them more to learn than to teach them about health. I remember old Mrs. Monise, who had an iron which she heated on an ancient coal stove, the only heat for her little shack. With that relic, she ironed her neighbor's clothes in exchange for food and coal. She had no money, but she had a joyous inner strength which she gave freely to all.

I, too, had some patients whose poverty seemed to magnify their innocence, and in that innocence was great wisdom. One older Hispanic man spoke prayers of gratitude in broken English whenever I entered the exam room to see him. He thanked me profusely for any little thing I said or did. It was true gratitude — and made my heart sing for the rest of the day.

I needed those gems to sustain me through the other side of poverty, the patients who were hardened and skilled at manipulating the welfare system for money and the health-care system for drugs or disability payments. In the beginning, I concentrated entirely on the spark of God burning within them, however dim it appeared on the outside. I loved these patients, and looked for openings to point out their good to them. Sometimes it was visibly received. Sometimes I couldn't tell what was going on by their lack of any visible reaction. But too often, they would plead and beg for drugs or disability papers, a glazed look covering their eyes, showing me how locked into this mode of operating they were. I knew they were really asking for love, not drugs or money, but without their openness or willingness, healing was not possible. Sometimes I gave them their drugs or disability papers, which deepened their sleepy state of consciousness. Sometimes I refused them what they wanted, which made them angrier. Sometimes I was pressured by a full waiting room of patients, occasionally arguing with each other or yelling abusive words at clinic staff. Sometimes I could keep my heart open and sometimes I couldn't. This went on for about a year.

Our family went on a vacation camping trip to our beloved Mt. Shasta. Sitting on the mountainside talking with Joyce about my county job, I became aware of a heaviness in my heart which contrasted sharply with the peace of my surroundings. In a moment of naked truth I realized that I needed to quit my job. Joyce and I held each other and gave thanks. The joy of that moment confirmed the rightness of the decision.

On my first day back to work, I announced my decision to leave my job. It was very hard, but it felt right.

I was still not done with medicine. A short time later I found myself creating the most ideal position possible with the county health department. I became medical director of a satellite clinic in a predominantly Hispanic town. Most of the patients were farm workers who spoke little or no English. I spoke very limited Spanish but felt I could bridge the language and cultural barriers by keeping my heart open. As director, I had added power and influence to create a more humanitarian and healing environment. I started staff meetings with meditations and relaxation techniques, and encouraged open communication. It took the whole clinic by surprise, staff and patients alike. They all thought I was *very* strange — but they liked me nevertheless.

Those first months were like a honeymoon period. "Dr. Love" had everyone hugging, patients as well as staff. But the harsh "realities" of a county health clinic finally sneaked up on all of us. "Dr. Love" was loving, but patients weren't seen fast enough and headquarters was complaining about possible repercussions, like loss of funding. Clinic staff stopped hugging and got tough again. Once again, efficiency and economy overruled compassion. The head won another battle over the heart.

Furthermore, no matter how hard I tried with my Hispanic patients, I could never quite bridge the cultural gap, except with a very few. There seemed to be some degree of reservation no matter how warm and loving I was. Perhaps it was me being a doctor just as much as me being a "gringo" doctor. Often I'd see the patients let go of their reserve when they were with Hispanic clinic staff after I'd seen them.

After about a year of trying to make this new job work, it was once again time for me to leave. I felt at a point of readiness to leave the complicated world of Western medicine. *The Shared Heart* had been published and we were receiving invitations from all over the country. My clinic was provided for — a good-natured Hispanic doctor was guided to me at the perfect time. I could leave the clinic in good hands...

I had three days to rejoice over my new-found freedom. Then the phone call came. It was Dr. Roy Howard, the director of student health at the university, offering me a permanent half-time position taking care of college students' health needs. I had worked there in the past, filling in for other doctors, and had always felt more at home there than in any other medical setting. While on the phone, I had an unmistakable sinking feeling in the pit of my stomach and might have been tempted to decline the offer on the spot, but Dr. Howard insisted I not make any decision until I had a few days to think about it.

And what days those were! There were moments of torture as I struggled with the feeling that once again I was giving up my ideals. There were moments of temptation as I thought about the immediate acceptance I had been given by students, staff, and faculty. Then there was the temptation of a regular pay check, of paid vacations, sick leave, health benefits and especially, summers off to travel and give our talks and workshops.

Finally, too weary to think anymore, I realized I was, alas, still not done with medicine. Like dinner in the oven, I was impatiently opening the door every few minutes and taking it out to check it, only to realize it was not yet done. I, too, needed more cooking.

In the course of the next year, I knew I was making deep changes within myself. I sensed that this university health center job would be my weaning from traditional medicine. Somehow I knew this would be the stepping-off point of my medical career, and the beginning of something more suitable to my nature. As ideal as this job was, as ideal as any job could be, I knew from the beginning that it would be very temporary. The pace was somewhat slower. I had time to work on deeper levels with the students. Most of the staff accepted me for who I was. Yet I was still not free to work with patients in the way my heart was desiring. I was still expected to prescribe many different drugs. And there still were many days when the pace was anything but slow. I remember sometimes coming home with a feeling of sadness, a feeling that something vital was missing in this job. There was still that certain heaviness in my heart.

As the months went by, the popularity of *The Shared Heart* grew. Our travel and work with groups increased, and so did our commitment to the writing of our second book, *Models of Love*. My commitment to the university was waning rapidly, as was my interest in the world of traditional medicine.

In the beginning of 1986, Joyce and I realized our lives were too busy to finish writing and publishing our new book. At one point we realized something had to change to open up the time we needed. We prayed together to be shown what it was.

I didn't have to wait long. I knew inside that my "risk to be healed" was to leave this last medical position. I needed to finally take the leap of faith into being on my own. And, as sometimes happens when these inner decisions are made, the universe can provide immediate opportunities.

In a meeting a few days later with Dr. Howard, my boss, I noticed a tension in his face. We had barely sat down when he blurted out, "Barry, you just don't fit in here. You're like a square peg in a round hole."

Despite my having already made the decision to leave this job, a wave of sadness came over me. Tears came into my eyes as what seemed like ancient feelings washed through my being, feelings of not belonging, not fitting in, no matter how hard I tried. I felt as if I had come from some distant galaxy and had never quite learned to make earth my home.

My tears seemed to have had a deep effect on Dr. Howard. He had fully intended to keep this meeting professional and objective, but suddenly he was also Roy, with his own feelings and tears welling in his own eyes. The tension left his face as he spoke. "You know," he explained, "this has been one of the hardest decisions I have ever made. I've been struggling over it for months. Never have I felt so close to a colleague."

Now that the professional tension was broken, we hugged each other in silence. In that embrace, I allowed myself to feel the full expression of my human emotions. Even though I had already decided to end my formal medical career, I still felt feelings of failure.

Still holding each other, Roy added in a gentle and sincere tone, "It's very strange, but something happened a few days ago. As I was struggling with this decision and putting it off once again, I had the strongest feeling that I would be doing you a very great favor to send you away from here. I felt...and feel...that you have other work to do."

I remembered the prayer Joyce and I spoke a few days before — perhaps at the same moment that Roy received his decision. I remembered how he spoke of *The Shared Heart* in front of the clinic staff, describing it as "filled with love." I remembered the joy in his voice when I accepted his job offer.

I felt now the hands of the Father-God holding me through this man in front of me. I felt the love and wisdom of the Divine Presence in full command, and Roy and I in our human selves were like puppets on strings going through the motions directed by our Real Selves. I felt this day was ending fourteen years of traditional medical practice. I might have continued working at the university months before acting on my decision to leave. I might have rationalized that I needed to finish this or that project, or that I needed to take extra time to prepare for leaving, or that I needed to make sure I would have enough of an income on my own. But no. The Great Presence was immediately "promoting" me to a new position.

A wave of joy and freedom was rising in my being. I started thanking Roy. He smiled, then a sad and wistful look came across his face as he said, "I wish I had the courage to follow my heart as you are doing, to do what I love to do rather than what I should do." I responded, "Roy, you did what you had to do with me. You freed me to be who I am, and for that I thank you."

Echoes of another time and place were coming back to me, and the friend who had prophesied, "Your vocation will someday become your vacation, and your vacation will become your vocation." I knew a major graduation, a real initiation, was now occurring in Dr. Howard's office. The work I *had* to do was merging with the work I *loved* to do. Vocation was merging with vacation.

A few short weeks later I was "unemployed," a word that means different things to different people. To me it meant freedom — not freedom from responsibility, but the freedom to be myself, and to work hard at it! In those first weeks and months, whenever I'd think about my leaving the world of traditional medicine I'd feel joy welling up within me, such a sweet confirmation that I was on the right track, that all this was God's gift to me.

The rest of that winter and spring of 1986 Joyce and I focused all our free time and energy on finishing *Models Of Love*. In the last weeks it was a day and night effort. Beth, our typist, practically lived with us. Our computer hummed continuously, while editors and proofreaders streamed in and out of our house. I sometimes smiled at the memory of our prayer that we be given the time to finish this book, and how quickly it was answered!

Many parts of my work have been anything but glamorous. Book publishing, promotion, setting up talks and workshops, and running a business office have been quite time-consuming. It is the tedious, behind-the-scenes aspect of our work. Even so, it is much more fulfilling than were so many parts of my medical jobs. I feel a living connection between the paper work, the phone calls, and the opening of people's hearts to love, whether through our written words or through counseling sessions or group work. Also, I feel I need to master and fully understand this behind-the-scenes work before I can let others step in and take over.

Invitations to give talks and workshops have increased dramatically since my leaving medicine. It is just as if the universe is filling in the vacant time-slots.

It is such a joy to work side-by-side with Joyce, especially in our work with groups. I enjoy the times when I can sit back and watch her radiate love and wisdom. It hasn't always been that way. I remember first starting out together with groups. I had all my experience from psychiatry and wholistic psychotherapy training. Joyce was "my wife" and "assistant." When she spoke or led some part of the group, I was sometimes tense or wished I was doing it. Over the years, her training has been to listen more and more deeply to the voice of her heart. Of course mine has been the same, but I have also had to unlearn all my left-brain material, the academic side of therapy. When Joyce now speaks, I am sometimes in awe and always appreciative.

If you have built castles in the air, your work need not be lost.
That is where they should be.
Now put the foundations under them.

HENRY DAVID THOREAU

Almost a year has passed since I had written the above stories and thoughts. Somehow, this chapter got put aside. The Great Editor-in-Chief is in charge of all our writing, and sometimes tables our work. It is now May 1988, over two years since my exodus from traditional medicine.

Last month, during a visit with my parents, they were talking with one of our friends in Santa Cruz. Something this friend said brought up a little sadness in my mom. Although she knew I was happier and more fulfilled now than ever before, there was still a part of her that was holding on to the identity of "her son, the doctor," and that part was grieving a perceived loss. She asked our friend if she thought I would ever be a doctor again. "Barry hasn't ever stopped being a doctor," our friend joyfully replied. "He's gone from being a doctor of the body to a doctor of the soul." My mom later told me that our friend's observations had brought her great joy, and had dispelled her last remaining doubts about my "career."

I am reflecting now on our teacher's prophecy, "Your vocation will become your vacation and your vacation will become your vocation." I realize that the vacation to which he was referring was not the usual image people have of vacation, for example, lying on a lounge chair in the sun, sipping on a cool drink. He was, instead, telling me that my work would be my greatest joy and that joy would be my greatest work. Yes, that my actual work in the world would be to bring joy to people's hearts. And *that* is healing.

We may be tempted to think that making our vocation our vacation means we will work less, if at all. There is an inherent laziness built into the human condition. We know some people who have quit their jobs, who have decided that they didn't want to work anymore, that work was a waste of precious time. Some are living off of savings. Others are getting by with the absolute minimum of work to sustain their basic needs. All of them desire to make their lives easier, feeling that God intends life to be easy. But none of them are happy or fulfilled. Instead, they seem to be floundering in life.

God, our Higher Self, does intend our lives to have "ease." Spirit-filled hard work is full of "ease," but is not necessarily easy. I look at my life right now and realize I'm working so much more than ever before, but because my work is so much more an expression of my heart, there is so much more "ease." Look at Mother Teresa. Sometimes people's first impression upon meeting her is how tired she looks. But does she feel tired? Perhaps, but mostly she is filled with the joy of serving the poor.

We also have to be careful of the reverse which says, "the harder we work and the more we accomplish, the happier we'll be." Many of us, including me, have the "workaholic" tendency. There is a saying that "being busy creates the illusion of purpose." The busier we are, the more fulfilled we must be. Right? Not quite. Keeping ourselves overly busy is an unconscious way of distracting ourselves from our real mission in life: to express our love. If alcoholism is the abuse of alcohol in an attempt to run away from ourselves, workaholism is the abuse of work in a similar attempt to escape.

What is the "workaholic" part of all of us running away from? If we're running away from the pain and suffering we have caused ourselves and others, then we need to stop and give love and forgiveness to ourselves for our unconsciousness. If we're running away from love because of a feeling of unworthiness, then we need to stop and remember who we are: children of the Creator, Sons and Daughters of the Light, rightful heirs to all the love and power of the universe.

Our message is not to quit your job. Nor is it to work for yourself rather than someone else. Making your vocation your vacation means bringing joy into whatever you do. My brother sells shoes in Minneapolis. Each person who comes into the store to try on a pair of shoes first gets a thorough foot-massage. This way, the customer's feet are relaxed and it's easier to fit the right pair of shoes. That's just the surface reason. My brother is really a healer. People come in to buy shoes from him because they want the foot massage. I know. I've experienced his massages! And that's what brings him joy — more than just selling shoes.

Sometimes the greatest risk is to keep doing the work you're doing but to find ways to bring more joy into it. And sometimes the greatest risk is to quit. In a counseling session with a couple, their big issue was his job. He traveled around the country leading workshops for a well-known organization. He loved his work and was good at it. He brought joy and growth into many lives. But there was another side to his job. He was away from his wife and children more than he was home. And there were pressures put on him from the administrative level of the organization. He loved his work, but hated the organization...and sorely missed his family.

In that counseling session it became clear that he needed to quit. With that realization came a surge of joy, which always follows a harmonious decision. They left very grateful.

A year passed. We never heard from them. It turns out that he never did quit his job because he got scared. Then they showed up at a weekend couple's retreat we were leading. They looked extremely pale and he especially looked tense. They shared with us that they really needed this retreat.

On Sunday morning, they went into the middle of the circle and asked the group for help. He asked to be supported in his decision to quit his job. This time we knew he was ready. His whole body shook with sobbing as he revealed his desire to be a husband and father. Another man came into the center and put his arm around this man and said, with a sincerity that spoke of long personal experience, "You won't miss the hotel rooms." He did finally quit, and a wonderful work gradually opened up for him and his wife.

When we close a door that is needing to be closed, the universe opens an even better one. We need to trust that we are being lovingly watched over and guided into the perfect work in this world.

We also need to be willing to let the outward expression of our work change as we change, to grow as we grow. We are constantly growing and changing. To expect that our work will remain the same is to deny this process. Certain jobs or careers are there to teach us lessons. When we learn the lessons, we need to allow our job or career to evolve. Again, it doesn't necessarily mean quitting. There may be ways to bring growth and change into our present work or job. Sometimes the greatest risk is to stay in a job and transform it from within. It's just like a relationship. When we get to a point of wanting to quit a relationship, leaving may not be the answer. Especially if we're feeling hurt and resentful, leaving can then be a reactive move. We may very well need some space to work through our feelings, but ultimately we need to feel our heart connection with this person before we can make a final decision about separation or divorce. It is in the peace of loving that we can hear our inner guidance.

It's the same with a job. Leaving with a bitter feeling is usually a poor time to leave. Better to take a vacation or leave of absence than to quit in a reactive mode. The time to quit (or move on) is when we can feel appreciation for the lessons learned in this job. Not just work lessons, but personal growth lessons as well. It is in the peace of appreciation for all that this job has brought to us that we will hear the truth within our hearts about what we need to do.

At the time of my greatest struggle with my transition from "vocation to vacation," a friend asked me, "Can you trust that you will be supported by following your heart?" If I was doing God's will, which was really *my* highest will, wouldn't I be supported by the universe?

What was the work my heart was leading me to do? It starts with the first commandment. It is "to love God (and myself) with all my heart." It is to love Joyce and the girls so that together we can become "models of love" for others. And it is "to love my neighbors as myself." It is to continue writing, for if it brings so much joy to me, then how could it not bring that same joy to others. And my work is beside Joyce in the workshops and retreats, for it is there that I experience the contagion of joy. It is there that I witness miracle after miracle of healing. It is there that I sing and dance with my brothers and sisters to the glory of God.

In the end, our vocation can only become our vacation if our focus is on divine service. If we ask ourselves, "Is my work helping to bring healing and peace on this planet?", and the answer is "yes", then vocation is merging with vacation.

If we could but remember standing on the threshold of our birth into this life, having been lovingly trained by our teachers and guides in the higher realms, we would also remember the joy we felt in anticipation of giving as we have been given to. Yes, we would remember the ecstasy in anticipation of serving, serving the earth, serving the people on it, serving God by being a Light-Worker.

In the end, it is loving by serving and serving by loving that is our true vocation.

When the time of our particular sunset comes,
our thing,
our accomplishments,
won't really matter a great deal.
But the clarity and care
with which we have loved others
will speak with vitality
of the great gift of life
we have been for each other.

BROTHER GREGORY, WESTON PRIORY

CHAPTER 7

Healing Beyond The Veil

The wise man never grieves over the dead or over the living, because he knows that God in His wisdom and compassion cares for all of His creatures. How can we ever find adequate words to truly convey to the anxious heart of man the rich love, the transcendent beauty and the enduring peace of God?

WHITE EAGLE

IN *SUNRISE*

HEN I WAS EIGHT YEARS OLD, I became convinced that my grandfather did not like me very much.

He always gave my parents a nice sum of money for our family for Christmas, but this year was a little different. He was also giving my older brother, Bruce, and me a separate envelope. I opened my envelope in eager expectation. I was just beginning to learn about money and was saving for a special doll. My envelope held five dollars. I glanced over at my brother as he pulled out ten dollars. Jealousy tore at my heart. My grandfather probably thought my twelve-year-old brother needed the money more than I, but to my child's way of reasoning it was a sure sign that he loved my brother more. My brother was extremely intelligent, interesting, funny, and easy to talk to. I was shy and emotional which, for some people, camouflaged my intelligence. I can now understand why my grandfather must have found it easier to be with Bruce than with me, but as a child I simply felt I wasn't loved by him. I began looking for evidence to support my feelings, and of course to a child any small action becomes proof.

My grandfather lived at our home during his ninety-second year. I was eighteen years old and had just fallen in love with Barry. I was home from college after my first year and my only thought was how I could visit with Barry who lived four hundred miles away. I spent long hours alone writing love letters and knitting him a sweater.

One morning I came down for breakfast and noticed my parents were red-eyed and looked very tired. "We were up all night sitting with your grandfather while he was dying," my mother said. "They just took his body away."

My mind was still stuck in my child's view of him. Though I loved him, I didn't show much emotion or feeling over his death. Right after the funeral I went to a party. As I danced and laughed with my friends that night, I tried then, and in the days and weeks ahead, to dance away from all memory of my grandfather. I might have succeeded except that my mother chose to keep his old walking cane in the closet right where he always hung it when he came to visit us. Every time I'd see the cane, I would tenderly touch it and warmth would stir within my heart. But I didn't understand these feelings and tried to push them aside in an attempt to maintain the separation from him that I had felt as a child.

Eleven years later and pregnant with Rami, I began earnestly seeking the guidance and inspiration of the higher beings and angelic presences. I wanted to learn from my unborn baby's teachers and guides. Each time I sat with this intention, I would immediately feel the presence of my grandfather. "Go away! I don't want you," I would say at first, and then instantly my meditation would end. Further attempts that day to meditate were fruitless.

After several weeks of this same pattern, I began to feel frustrated. I could go only so far in meditation, to the point of just sensing the higher spheres and then, abruptly, there was my grandfather's presence. My rejection of him then ended my attempt at meditation.

Finally I realized that I needed to open to my grandfather's spirit rather than continue pushing him away. During my next meditation, I did just that. My narrow view of him melted away as I saw him reaching out to me with love and protection. "What a beautiful soul he is," I thought.

Fond memories began to flood my being. There were times in my life when he had reached out in love to me and I hadn't noticed. I remembered the mornings he would stay in his room before breakfast creating a little story he could tell me in German, his native language, to help with my German studies. Rather than sensing the thoughtfulness in his action, I had felt frustrated because German was my hardest subject in school and I couldn't understand the story. There were many other incidents in which he had shown his love in his own way. I just hadn't seen it at the time.

Forgiveness flowed from my heart, both for my grandfather and for myself in my blindness. I felt how strong our connection of love really was. With that realization, he seemed to take me by the hand to a place of higher inspiration. I realized that in my attempt to feel God, I could not bypass healing my relationships with those in the spirit world.

Many persons desiring spiritual growth are aware that their hearts cannot be fully open to others as long as they are closed to even one person. In the act of forgiving and opening to that one person they open to all beings. Many people do not realize, however, that this same truth also applies to our relationship with those in the spirit world. If we hold a painful or negative memory of someone who has passed on, or simply don't want to ever think of that person again, we are correspondingly holding back our own growth. In our attempts to rise in consciousness and feel the ever-loving arms of God, if there is a part of us withholding love from one of God's children we can never reach our goal. And those in the spirit world are part of God's family.

In my attempt to block my grandfather from my memory, I was actually closing the door to higher consciousness. Long after I had forgotten that I had been the one to close the door, I felt frustrated in my attempt to open it once again. As I had closed it through choosing to experience the negative, I could open it by choosing to experience the good. I was surprised to find that the good far out-weighed the negative, which I had mostly *imagined*. Through opening the door I was delighted to find such a beautiful soul, loving me and willing to give support and encouragement for the remainder of my life. I don't dwell on thoughts of my grandfather, but every once in a while a memory will come or a feeling of his presence, and I know that I now have a true friend in the spirit world, someone who is cheering my every attempt at growth. I still touch his old walking cane, and the warmth that stirs within my heart brings sweet tears to my eyes.

Taking the risk to heal relationships with those in the spirit world can affect many different aspects of life. When we hold anger, resentment or guilt feelings towards those we have known who have passed on, it becomes a poison which slowly filters into all areas of our life. Long after the person is forgotten from conscious memory, the poison from the negative feelings remains, coloring the way we respond to life's experiences and obstructing our own process of opening and healing.

I shall never forget a workshop where two courageous people took giant steps in healing across the veil between life and death. This particular workshop was intense and powerful from the very first night. All of the twenty people present were sensitive and wanted to work on healing themselves and others. Towards the end of the first day I noticed that Janice, a woman in the back of the room, was becoming increasingly agitated. I also noticed that her husband was giving her support to come to the center of the room. I asked Janice to come forward. Without moving she blurted out, "I just know I'm supposed to heal my relationship with my mother, but I don't know where to begin and I feel scared."

With encouragement from the group Janice sat in the middle and began to unravel her story. She had been the oldest of four children. Her mother had been in and out of mental hospitals for many years, and since Janice was the eldest, she was expected to care for her younger siblings and the house while her mother was away. When not in the hospital her mother tended to take out her anger and crazy behaviors on Janice.

When Janice became an adolescent, her mother made several suicide attempts and the hospitalization periods became longer. Because of her many responsibilities and duties at home, Janice had little time for dating or social life. In her senior year of high school she finally started dating a nice boy and they made plans to go to the senior prom. This was the biggest event to which she had ever been invited. Janice started preparing for the prom weeks ahead of time. As her excitement grew, her mother, who was home from the hospital, grew increasingly depressed and insisted that her daughter not go to the prom. For the first time in her life, Janice stood up for what she knew was right and fair. She happily continued making plans to go.

The night of the prom came. She donned the dress she had carefully made by herself. Brushing her hair in a fancy style, she felt free and independent for the first time in her life. Her boyfriend came and off they went to the prom. She was having a marvelous time at the prom, feeling happier than she had ever felt when an urgent announcement came over the loudspeaker for her. Going to the front stage the bandmaster grimly told her the news that her mother had just killed herself. Janice stomped her foot and marched out of the room in a rage. Within minutes all her friends had heard the news and wondered why she had responded with anger rather than sadness.

On her way home Janice felt like kicking her mother's dead body. "Why did she choose this special night to do this? Surely she planned this to spoil my fun and happiness," the girl thought. The anger remained throughout the funeral and became a poison which infiltrated every area of her life.

Janice later married, had four children, and developed a successful career. However, she felt unfulfilled in her job, ineffectual in her role as a mother, and her marriage was threatening to dissolve.

"Could all this be related in some way to my feelings of hatred and anger towards my mother?" she asked. We knew that to some degree there had to be a relationship.

Some participants in the workshop felt that the woman had every right to feel anger towards her mother. They felt that she should express her anger all the more. To us, however, it was obvious that Janice had expressed her anger over and over again, and it had become a large festering wound which weakened every fiber of her being. The anger had been expressed, but the deeper feelings of abandonment, hurt, fear, and behind these, love...yes, love...had yet to be experienced. Often it is easier for us to express emotions of rage, anger and resentment. We feel justified in having these feelings, that somehow we are right because of all the wrong that has been done to us. In time, however, we see how we ourselves are the creators of our reality, that the God within us chooses the situation that will bring about the most soul growth for us. We forget this, however. The anger is a cover-up for the pain and fear, and the pain and fear, in turn, hide the love, our original intention and desire.

In order to experience love, fulfillment, and happiness in our lives, we must be willing to love and forgive others. We cannot feel the joy of fully opening to life when there is even one person to whom we are closed. There is a Sufi saying: "If there is room in your heart for one enemy, your heart is not a safe place for a friend." Whatever the seeming injustice, we are asked to look into the deepest core of our being and feel love and forgiveness.

We asked Janice to pick out someone in the room who reminded her of her mother. Right away she picked out a woman who we later found out was also having trouble forgiving her mother. We asked Janice to hold this woman as if she were holding her own mother. We asked her to feel the motherly feelings of compassion, caring, nurturing and love towards her own mother, by remembering the buried tender moments and the hidden beautiful qualities her mother possessed. This was very hard for Janice since she had carried many years of resentful and angry feelings within her. The group moved closer and lent their strength and healing energies.

At first each slightly positive memory or thought was immediately followed by a negative one. Then there came one positive memory in which Janice truly felt the flow of love between her mother and herself. With this small but significant feeling of compassion, a flood of warm feelings was released. Janice burst into tears as the grief over the loss of her mother surfaced for the first time. She told her mother that even though it had been a difficult relationship, she had loved her and wanted her to stay.

After a while we asked her to close her eyes and imagine her mother standing right by her side. Janice then described the radiant form of her mother, with arms outstretched loving her. She remembered a poem her mother had written her as a little girl. The poem expressed her mother's deep love for Janice, and also her own struggle to remain in a world that seemed so harsh. Janice saw that the love her mother had so beautifully expressed in that poem had never died and would always be there for her to receive. By experiencing her love for her mother rather than hatred, she had opened a golden door to receive the good and beautiful. This experience of love changed the poison to a sweet nectar which would add strength and healing to her life.

Janice was needing to change *her* concept of her mother. When she could experience her mother's radiance in the spirit world, she was also able to receive her love. By concentrating on even the smallest expression of love...the poem her mother wrote for her...she was able to bring her attention to her mother's love and thus open the door to experiencing her mother's soul essence. By drawing our attention to even the most insignificant positive memory and then expanding on that, we are able to eventually experience the totality of good in another. As one of our beloved teachers repeatedly told us, "What your attention is upon you become."

Janice's face glowed with light and love. She was the picture of serenity. "What a perfect feeling to close our afternoon session," I thought as I glanced at my watch and noticed it was dinner time. The other members of the group had been so involved in Janice's process that they also had a look of deep peace upon their faces. I was ready to close the session when William raised his hand. William had sat on the periphery of the group all during the workshop. He seemed slightly disinterested in all that was going on, usually choosing to sit back towards the wall when the rest of us were in the middle. He had not responded to our efforts to include him. Now I noticed he had crept closer to the center and wanted to speak. "Something came up for me while Janice was forgiving her mother," he faltered and looked around at the rest of the group. "I know you are all ready for dinner but my mother also committed suicide. I haven't even let myself think of her until just now. Do you think I could be helped too?"

Our group instantly responded to William and made space for him in the middle. Dinner could wait.

William told how his mother had committed suicide twelve years ago when he was twenty-one years old. He was the one who had found her dead body hanging on a rope. As he was taking his mother down he told her that he loved her. As he placed her body on the floor he started to cry, but then stopped himself. After the funeral he forced himself never to think about her again. This might have continued except that Janice's experience brought the whole incident to his mind again.

We asked Janice to be his mother and had William hold her in his arms. We then asked William to speak to Janice as if she were his mother. "I love you, mother," he said in a flat, monotone voice. Janice, from her recent healing experience, was very sensitive to William and coached, "You are saying words without feeling." Again he tried. Again Janice told him she felt no feeling behind his words. He tried again and again in his monotone voice to express himself. Finally Janice looked at him intently and said, "William, feel! I am your mother!"

Suddenly he clutched his heart with his hands and cried out in pain. For a moment everyone thought he was having a heart attack. Then we realized that he was perceiving painful sensations in his heart, having closed it to his mother for twelve years. Now his heart was opening. His monotone voice gave way to deep expression of feeling, "Oh Mother, I loved you so much, why did you leave me?" As he cradled his mother in his arms, he expressed his love and sorrow. Then he added, "You named me William after your departed father. I always felt like I was your father." Clutching his heart even tighter he sobbed, "When you killed yourself I felt like it was all my fault because I hadn't been a good enough father to you."

As he cried our group comforted him. Finally the guilt that had caused so much darkness and contraction was let go. Now the light of God was illuminating the darkness and healing the wound.

I asked William to feel his mother's presence in the room with him and imagine what she would be saying. He closed his eyes and smiled, "She loves me very much and says her act of suicide had *nothing* to do with me. She is even saying that it was my love and constant concern for her that kept her alive for twenty-one years. "Oh Mother, I love you!" His face melted into ecstasy, as communion between mother and son was once again possible.

All the while he kept rubbing his heart. Finally he opened his eyes and announced, "My heart feels good! There is a nice feeling there. I have had chest and back pain ever since my mother died. My back feels better too!" A chiropractor in the group explained that the upper back pain he'd been experiencing was probably directly related to the contracted condition of his heart. Though it was painful at first to open to all the stored up feelings, the opening eventually brought great joy. William and Janice hugged each other. As we gazed upon them we were all grateful for God's healing touch in our group.

Healing relationships with those in the spirit world, especially a parent, is always one of my favorite parts of a workshop. I do not see spirit bodies, nor do I hear their verbal messages, but I can feel their loving presence. The love deceased parents have for their living child is very real. I find myself sometimes intoxicated by this beauty and sweetness.

When parents first hold their newborn child, they are given the spiritual gifts of devotion and commitment. Although sometimes these gifts are not consciously felt, most of the time the parent feels in this moment that there is nothing they wouldn't do for their child.

People scoff at this idea. They argue that it might be true for other parents, but certainly their own parent never held such commitment and devotion. Yet we only have to observe the commitment of every mother animal for her newborn to know that the same God-force or instinct is in every human parent. When Barry was in medical school, the first baby he helped deliver was from a woman who screamed throughout the labor, "I don't want this baby!" Yet when the infant was born and then handed to its reluctant mother, this woman held her baby close to her and started crying. The instinctual mother-child bond of love could be felt by everyone in the room. True, in the stress of life, the commitment of parent to child may seem to be clouded. Children may then conclude that their parent is not very devoted to them. However, as soon as that parent leaves their body at death, the stress of physical life dissolves and their commitment and devotion to their children come to the forefront. It is then one of their greatest desires to give their love to their child. Whenever there is an opportunity to express their love, whenever a child on earth opens his heart to his parent in the spirit world, this parent is fully present to communicate their caring. I find these times so blissful, when the bridge of light between the heaven world and the earth is made. I feel like bathing myself in the love parents have for their child.

It is so powerful when an individual creates a bridge by allowing in the love of their deceased parent on a daily basis. This does not mean that we need to obsess on thoughts of our parent. Just a loving thought, a daily remembrance of warmth, can establish a permanent flow of love. Many people have reported to me that their relationship with their parent actually grew deeper after that parent had died. My own mother, whose mother died when she was seven years old, continually tells me that her mother has never left her side and continues to help and love her. People who have had near death experiences usually report that it is their parent in the land of light who first welcomes them to their new home and then points the way to the light. It is as if the parent who has passed on continues to be committed to their child until that child enters the spirit world and is once again home in the light. To reject this very personal love because of hurt or anger is to miss a tremendous blessing and source of strength in your life.

People often wonder, "What about the injustice and pain *we* have caused those who are now crossed over to the world of light?"

I shall never forget a workshop we led in Southern England. The workshop seemed to go quite slowly the first day. The English seemed a little confused about what these sometimes outrageous Americans were having them do. We, on the other hand, wondered why tea time was so very important. But by the next day the English were more used to our ways, and we were already looking forward to the afternoon tea.

I led a meditation to connect people with those loved ones who had passed on. At the close of the meditation Barry noticed Francis, a young man, who was softly crying. Barry urged him to come forward. After much quiet resistance, Francis sat in the center of our circle. We all immediately liked his quiet, gentle and humble manner. We asked Francis to share his story. He replied that he couldn't, feeling that if he did, no one in the room would be able to ever like him again. People sat closer and assured him that no matter what he shared they would still continue to like him. There was such a presence of love and acceptance in the room that Francis took the risk to share.

He began very tentatively, as if testing us in our ability to love him. "I had always wanted to be a nurse working with psychiatric patients. When I was accepted in the program I was elated. I felt I could really help those with mental confusion and sickness. At first I threw myself into the work with full enthusiasm. I loved working with the psychiatric patients and they all loved me. I also had a girl friend whom I adored more than anyone in the world. She was the daughter of an important foreign diplomat and I could hardly believe she wanted to be with me. I felt deep devotion for her. Then everything started to change. I started to feel a great power surging through me, a sense that I could do great and wonderful things. By itself, that was fine, but I started to take it further. I began feeling that I was Jesus Christ.

Healing Beyond The Veil 135

"At first this was a beautiful feeling and I felt tremendous love flow through me to the patients. They supported my feeling and told me I looked like Jesus. I became their Christ and I loved it.

"Then came the paranoid feelings about the hospital staff. I became increasingly convinced that they were plotting to crucify me. Over the next few weeks I became more and more scared. I trusted no one but my precious girlfriend. She became my confidante, the only one I talked to or cared about.

"In an attempt to get away from my 'assassins' at work, I quit my job. My closest friends noticed the change in me and urged me to seek help. I became convinced that they too were in on the plot to crucify me. I would now see no one but my beloved.

"While out driving one day, I was stopped for speeding. The officer asked who I was and where I was going. I told him I was Jesus Christ going to Jerusalem. He handed me a slip of paper asking me to report to a psychiatric facility the next morning. I was sure that this was the sign that Good Friday had come and my time was at hand.

"I drove with my girlfriend to the Isle of Wight, hoping I would be safe there. We arrived at the house of a woman whom I respected highly. She welcomed us in her home but expressed some concern about my condition. It was late and, as we settled into a bedroom, my friend determined to wait out the night and call the police in the morning.

"As we lay down to sleep my girlfriend innocently asked why I seemed to be running away. In that instant my mind totally flipped and I saw my beloved as part of the plot to crucify me. I grabbed her. She struggled...and I strangled her to death."

Tears flowed as Francis spoke the final words and he covered his face in shame. His whole body was wet from nervous perspiration. There was a breathless silence in the room. One by one, people gently placed their hands on Francis and expressed their love. Here was a man who had just admitted to psychosis and murder, yet the feeling of love and forgiveness from the rest of the group was absolutely awesome. Even people who had no experience with mental illness had total compassion for him.

Francis further explained with face covered that he had been brought to a mental hospital where he spent eight years recovering.

Now he was allowed to be out under careful observation. We asked Francis to look into the faces of those around him. At first he said he couldn't, as his shame was so great. But when he did finally look he was amazed to see the love and understanding in people's faces. He found himself being loved unconditionally by everyone in the room.

We asked him to close his eyes and picture his beloved girlfriend. We asked him to imagine what she was wanting to communicate to him. He said he was convinced she utterly hated him. We urged him to try and really feel her and see her. Soft tears fell from his closed eyes as he finally said, "She looks lovelier than ever...she still loves me. Somehow she understands all that happened."

Francis's face shone with wonder and joy. After going through torment for eight years, he was now opening himself to love again. One woman in the group was noticeably touched by what was happening. She sat up straight, cleared her throat, and said in a soft, deliberate and reverent voice, "Now I know what heaven must be like. Heaven is experiencing God's total unconditional love and acceptance for us, just as we are all now feeling for Francis." There was a profound sense of peace in the room, a peace which we knew was working a healing magic on everyone present.

It is worth every effort to come into harmony with those in the spirit world. Remember that those in spirit are not the same as they were while in the body. In the non-material realm, the grievances they had on earth are more easily cast aside. They are now willing to meet us halfway. We need to let go of our old images of them and accept them for who they now are. Then we will be able to open to their love for us, feel our love for them in return, and thus experience the loving connection that has always been there. By doing this, we are building a bridge of light from earth to heaven, a bridge which helps to heal not only that one relationship, but all relationships. The resulting light of divine healing then becomes a great blessing for the whole planet.

> *The key-note of your life is love and service; as you love and serve God and man, you will radiate the light. Before you lies a path of never-ending progress. Do not let the heaviness of the world hold you down, but go forward as a pilgrim on the path of spiritual unfoldment.* — WHITE EAGLE IN *SUNRISE*

CHAPTER 8

The Risk to Appreciate

DURING MY YOUTH, I used to believe that saying something nice to someone was most often flattery. You usually said something nice when you wanted something from someone.

Then at age eighteen I found myself in a relationship with Joyce, and I entered a whole new world — the world of appreciation. Joyce was definitely more natural at it, so she became my teacher. Sometimes it felt good when she appreciated me. Sometimes it felt awful. I began to see that it felt good when I let it in, and not so good when I put up a shield.

I also learned the difference between flattery and true appreciation. When there are strings attached, it is not appreciation. It is wanting something. It is "conditional" loving. Early in our relationship, it was the difference between strings and ropes. Now it is more subtle. Now I go between strings and harder-to-spot threads. When there are no strings, or even threads, when all I want is to give the gift of my love in my words, *that* is true appreciation. And it always makes me happy as well as Joyce or whomever I am appreciating. I end up giving a great gift to myself. I am learning a law of appreciation: *The giver of unconditional appreciation receives by the very act of giving.*

It can also be a great risk to appreciate another. For to really appreciate, you must become vulnerable and open — unprotected. What if you open your heart and appreciate someone and they react negatively, or even worse, they don't react at all. This brings us to a second principle of appreciation: *You can't judge the effect of your appreciation by the other's response.*

When I was a third year medical student at USC in Los Angeles, Joyce and I had a friend a year ahead of me. One day, while he was visiting and we were sitting around our table, Joyce was bubbling up with appreciation for this man and started thanking him for his beauty, for his strength, and mostly for his being. He looked at her with a blank, expressionless stare, and then looked down at the table. Joyce felt strange and a little silly for being so enthusiastic — *and* so vulnerable. She felt she had just created tension rather than joy.

Six months later we were visiting this same friend, who was now in a psychiatric residency program. We had been together for some time when he faced Joyce and asked, "Remember the last time we were together and you appreciated me so deeply?", Joyce nodded. "Well," he continued, "I have been working with my therapist on the reactions I had to that moment ever since that day."

Joyce's appreciation had a profound effect on him. At the time, he was paralyzed with confusion, and thus the blank stare. Later, however, it brought up many feelings and much conflict. That simple but heart-felt appreciation catalyzed deep growth in his personal life.

A third truth about appreciation is this: *What you most appreciate in another is what is already present within you.* You may, however, be unaware of it. And also, when you appreciate those qualities in another, that very act helps to bring them out in you. Sometimes you are attracted to a certain quality in someone else which you feel you do not have yourself. However, you would not be attracted to that quality if it were not already present within you. Though you may be able to recognize it in others, you may be blind to it in yourself.

When Joyce and I were getting acquainted at the tender age of eighteen, I had a hard time with her exuberance and spontaneity. She walked down the street at our little up-state New York college town with an uninhibited child-like bounce. It made me very uncomfortable! I was trying very hard to be mature and sophisticated. Once I even crossed the street to walk on the other side, pretending I didn't know Joyce. The strange thing was that I was also *very* attracted to these qualities but struggled with it in my mind. My real nature (as my friends now know) is spontaneous, uninhibited, and sometimes impish. These qualities in me emerged as I acknowledged my attraction to them in Joyce, and began appreciating them in her.

Another rule of appreciation is this: *Use words as well as actions.* Many of us know how meaningless words can be when they're not followed up by actions. But have you considered that the reverse is equally true? Words of genuine appreciation mean more to many people than gifts or actions. It is easier to hide our loving feelings behind gifts and deeds than behind words, especially the spoken word. Speaking words of appreciation is a baring of the soul. Perhaps that's why we're sometimes afraid to use our words in such a vulnerable way.

Many of us are aware of the "chakras", energy centers of the body described by the esoteric sciences of both East and West. The voice and spoken word correspond to the "throat chakra," which lies between the forehead center above and the heart center below. The forehead center (the "third eye") is the center of the mind, also of vision. The heart center is the energy center of the body, the center of love and feeling. When I contemplate the throat center, I feel it is the place where, in its highest function, the mind and the heart join and can be expressed. So the spoken word can reflect the joining of both mind and heart.

We often begin workshops with appreciation. We have found that this centers participants in their hearts very quickly. Even if it's just a three-hour evening workshop, we pair people up, have them face each other and look for the greatest strength and the deepest beauty in one another. Then we ask them to share this in words.

The beauty that we see in another is really indescribable because it is the Divine shining through them which we are seeing. Sometimes we feel helpless in our use of words. We therefore feel tempted to not say anything rather than to fall short with our clumsy words. We need to know that it is our intentions which really matter, not the actual words. If our intention is to share our love, the clumsiness of our words will be less important than the feeling of the shared love.

---

142   *Risk To Be Healed*

Sometimes we chance upon the healing power of appreciation only in our despair. I'll never forget the story one couple told of a time in their relationship when their disharmony grew to enormous proportions. One day they realized that separation was immanent. They sank into despair. In this despair, however, they talked and decided they had not done all they could to save their marriage.

They decided upon one last experiment. Every day, without exception, they would pray together for strength, and then take turns appreciating each other. In the beginning, each appreciation felt contrived and superficial. "I liked the dinner you cooked" or "Your hair looks good today." Sometimes it was an extreme effort to say anything nice at all. In those times they felt filled with resentment and couldn't see anything positive about one another. However, it was their final try, and they had made a promise to each other to try this one last time. If it failed, they would then go their separate ways.

Then something wonderful started to happen. These regular "appreciation sessions" seemed to be gathering a momentum. The appreciations were deepening: "Your smile makes me happy" and "Thank you for loving me enough to try this experiment." The words began flowing more easily. The couple grew to look forward to their special time each day.

Years later, there they sat in front of the group, in as solid and loving a relationship as anyone could have. Perhaps it was their destiny to remain together, but we believe it was appreciation that uncovered that destiny.

Often people ask us (especially when we tell them we still argue), "What's the best way to end an argument?" We immediately respond "appreciation."

During our twenty-four years of arguing and studying our arguing, we have tried many different methods. We have tried outscreaming each other (the neighbors never enjoyed that method). We have tried leaving each other alone (eventually works, but can take a *long* time). We've tried being civilized, carefully communicating our grievances and then making sure we've been heard clearly (try being rational at totally irrational times). We've tried esoteric methods, like breathing practices, yoga asanas, this mantram, that affirmation, but again, in the heat and emotional upheaval of an argument, all these methods can easily get sabotaged. Then there's the obvious: Let go of your side. Give in. Surrender. How silly to be attached to your puny point of view. It's like the blind men and the elephant. One feels its tail and proclaims an elephant is a rope. Another feels its side and assures his comrades they are dealing with a wall. A third, discovering a leg, argues that an elephant is nothing more than a tree. Who is right. Everybody and nobody. But try to let someone tell you it's an animal when you're convinced it's a rope, when all your senses tell you one thing, and your mate tells you something else. Very difficult method!

Then there's appreciation — and prayer. Appreciation is often prayer in action or words. In the heat of an argument, we're only wanting to argue, so nothing will work. It's only when we come to the point of wanting to stop (and often time apart quickens that process) that any method can work. As long as there's the will to stop fighting, the way will be found. But we've discovered appreciation is the fastest for us. Prayer gives us the courage to take the risk to appreciate, and appreciation ends the argument.

After we've been arguing, our egos are more deeply invested in our particular image of the elephant, so it's always awkward in the beginning and the appreciations may be superficial at first (i.e. less threatening to voice). The important message here is to keep at it, because even lightweight appreciations will build a momentum. Joyce and I find that when the first smile breaks out on one of our faces, the end of the argument is close at hand. Then the appreciations deepen and the Divine Presence takes command. For whenever there is appreciation there is love, and when there is love there is no room to cling to personal opinions. We're not saying personal opinions cease to exist, but the clinging to them, the forceful hanging on, is replaced by a more graceful allowing.

Sometimes couples come to us for counseling who seem only to want to express anger. They want to scream and yell, blame and attack. They want to make sure *we* know how horrible a person their partner is. And they're convinced that this is all in the name of healing. We're not talking about people who are repressing their anger and for whom this kind of expression may be helpful. Rather, we are referring to couples for whom anger is the easiest option. They could spend the whole hour alternating between anger and quiet blame and judgment.

A few minutes into the session and we have the picture. We explain that we *will* come back to those issues which they revealed, but first they need to appreciate each other. We have them face each other and offer helpful starting suggestions like, "Remember when you first fell in love. What was it about this person that was the most beautiful? What quality attracted you the most?" It is a little sneaky to yank them into the past, but sometimes this kind of quick change of space is necessary.

One couple drove down from Marin (about two hours north of Santa Cruz) to see us. On the way they got into an argument. This is not an unusual occurrence. After all, they were trying to prepare for the session by bringing up their deepest unresolved issues. It then only requires one insensitive remark and the other feeling attacked and wounded, and the arena is set.

The arguing got so intense that they had to pull the car over onto the shoulder of the freeway. She spoke one final wounding blow to his ego and he went berserk. He grabbed her purse and threw it across the lanes of traffic. While she went running across the roadbed, dodging cars and trucks, he contemplated driving off and leaving her stranded, but managed to control this impulse. She came back with her purse, got into the back seat of the car, and neither of them said a word until they came into our house.

We took one look at them and knew we had our hands full. It didn't take long for the sparks to fly again between these two. Each told their own version of what had taken place on the freeway, each of their stories making the other look like a villain. Their hearts were so closed to each other that we knew talking about these issues would get us nowhere.

So we pulled out our "appreciation maneuver." As usual, there was extreme resistance at first. They thought it was some silly game that would waste the time which could be spent in "heavy processing." But it worked...and it worked fast. Within five minutes they were crying in each other's arms. The appreciating cut through the anger and distrust like a sword, revealing the deeper issues of which they were only barely aware, and which were the real reasons they were coming for a counseling session. These issues turned out to be fear of abandonment and fear of intimacy. We could then focus on these two, as well as other issues, without the defense of anger, and steps could be taken toward healing. Without the appreciation, and the breaking out of the anger-blame cycle, all of their time might have been used in yelling insults back and forth.

> *Anger cannot occur unless:*
> > *1) you believe you have been attacked*
> > *2) that your attack is justified in return and*
> > *3) that you are in no way responsible for it.*

A COURSE IN MIRACLES

A final pointer about appreciation: *Don't put it off.* Don't wait until you are "more together" or even in a better state of mind and emotions. *Do it now!*

After spending much of the Saturday of a weekend workshop working on unresolved issues with our parents, a woman realized she needed to heal a grudge she'd been holding toward her mother for many years. Her first temptation was to put off the phone call she knew she needed to make until she felt stronger in her love. The last thing we said on that Saturday to the group was "Do it now!" Sunday morning, before coming to the workshop, she telephoned her mother. Imagine how happy her mother was to hear words of love, gratitude, appreciation, and a sincere reaching out for forgiveness. Then her mother grew serious and said, "Tomorrow morning I go to the hospital for surgery. I have cancer." Even on the phone, the shared tears of a mother and daughter, estranged from each other by some misunderstanding, provided a miraculous healing of two people. This woman's mother died during the operation the next day! And we in the workshop learned a little more about the shortness and preciousness of human life. We cannot take our relationships for granted and assume we have all the time in the world to take the healing steps we need.

So if there is someone in your life whom you have not appreciated in a while, perhaps someone with whom there has been misunderstanding, or someone you love deeply and simply have not taken the time to appreciate, don't put it off any longer. Take the risk to appreciate — the risk to be healed. And do it now!

CHAPTER 9

The Risk to Embrace Pain

It is the darkest nights that prepare the greatest dawns.

SRI AUROBINDO

CHRISTMAS IS MY FAVORITE TIME OF YEAR. Since childhood I have always delighted in its customs and meaning. I have fond memories of being an angel in one Christmas play and being too shy to walk out on stage. The congregation saw a manger scene followed by a little girl being pushed toward the center from off stage. They saw her stumble, almost fall and finally say in a wee small voice, "I bring you great tidings of joy."

Christmas meant fun. As a small child I remember going to Aunt Gertrude's house and joining with my other girl cousins. We were all dressed up in our new Christmas dresses and took great delight in modeling, not the new velvet dresses, but the pretty slips underneath. As my mother was one of eight children, I always had an abundance of cousins, aunts and uncles to admire my new slip.

Christmas meant making things for others and giving little surprises. Many a night in December my parents would wake up with crumbs in their bed from a hand-decorated cookie I had lovingly tucked under their pillow.

No matter what the family situation, my enthusiasm about the Christmas season prevailed over all. One year, while in my early teens, my mother sadly announced to my brother and I that due to a change in our family's financial situation there would be no extra money for Christmas presents. We were each allowed to pick out a winter coat that we needed and that would be saved as our only Christmas present. The feeling of sadness which pervaded our family's Christmas preparation was more than I could bear, so I secretly plotted ways to create a joyful Christmas. I refused to think that Christmas could be less joyful just because there wasn't the money for presents. I knitted my mother a pair of mittens and sewed a scarf for my dad and brother.

Then came the fun! I spent days planning a treasure hunt for each member of the family to follow to find their presents. Some clues were very hard and others were very silly. My parents worried that I was spending so much time alone because I was sad about Christmas. Not so! I was never more excited!

On Christmas morning our family met at the tree as we had for each year since my brother and I had been born. Rather than the usual pile of gifts, there were two boxes containing our coats. I could tell my parents felt badly. I could have cared less as I handed them each their first "clue." For an hour the house rang with laughter as everyone raced about hunting down their treasures. Afterwards we all agreed. It had been the best Christmas of all!

One year, while in high school, I baked forty different kinds of Christmas cookies. It took our family a year to eat them all. Advent calendars, home made candles and cards, decorating the house, Christmas caroling in the snow and making all my gifts, brought so much joy and love to my growing up years.

Then I became an adult. I married and moved far away from my childhood home. Christmas was just not the same. The demands and responsibilities of adult life seemed to often crowd out the Christmas magic. Studying for exams, paying bills and nurturing my new relationship with Barry seemed to take all of my interest and attention. My enthusiasm for Christmas waned, and gradually I began to dread my beloved season. Rather than joy, I often felt sad remembering how Christmas used to be. I gave more attention to any sad or stressful events in my life than to the joy of the season. It was difficult to feel the same spirit I had enjoyed while growing up.

In this period of my late twenties I began to grow spiritually and realize the inner meaning of Christmas. Gradually, year by year, I saw that my joy could be returned by concentrating on the birth of the Christ Light within my heart. My highest act of giving became making myself a vessel for this light — giving myself to God. My vision of Christmas expanded as I sensed the lasting joy of spirit that could continue throughout the year. I focused each Christmas season on attaining this inner spirit and inspiration.

As sincere and devoted as I was in this practice, something always seemed to test me. On many occasions I was unable to hold to the inner joy, and so I experienced suffering. One year, when Rami was six years old and first really aware of Santa Claus, she came out on Christmas morning and beheld her presents. Her face briefly held wonder and then pain as she threw up all over our living room. She was so sick she couldn't open her presents for four days.

The next year was my turn. I got bronchitis and spent most of the Christmas holiday coughing and gargling salt water. The following Christmas I had to have very painful dental surgery and spent Christmas with my face wrapped in ice packs. A year later I had a full case of pneumonia and spent Christmas with a high fever. Last year at Christmas we learned our unborn baby had died. Rather than joyful celebration, I went in for surgery to remove her body, and then began a long grieving process.

This year, 1987, I was more determined than ever that I would experience a joyful Christmas. I began months ahead of time to prepare for this meaningful time. I studied past Christmases and took preventive measures. I had my teeth checked. I began building my body in a strong healthy way by running 45 minutes a day, eating the purest of foods and getting plenty of rest. I prepared spiritually by rising early each morning and meditating upon the inner meaning of Christmas. I prepared with the children by reading stories of the Nativity, making teddy bears as gifts for special loved ones, dipping beeswax candles and decorating them, making cards, and totally transforming our house with red and green delights. Christmas music filled our home, as did the excitement of Rami and Mira. I felt so much joy I could have burst.

One week before Christmas I sat with Barry before the girls woke up. It was a cold, stormy day but I felt filled with enthusiasm.

"Barry, I believe I've been able this year to recapture the joy of my childhood Christmases and bring that into my adult mind and heart."

Barry smiled and hugged me. Being raised Jewish, he could never quite understand my disappointment over the lack of Christmas joy. He experienced the newness of each year's Christmas and delighted in learning the carols and going to the concerts. Having nothing with which to compare it as a child, he accepted it all with gratefulness. Christmas has always been special, but no big deal to him. He has patiently observed my quest for the "lost Christmas joy."

I danced around the room. When the girls woke up I put on "Joy to the World" and we danced around the tree. Joy, joy, how I love JOY!!

A while later Barry left for the office with Mira who would first be dropped off at her Waldorf kindergarten. I prepared Rami's homeschool lessons while she practiced her guitar. Today we only planned to work for one hour and then spend the rest of the day finishing our Christmas presents. I decided to take our dog for a little walk while waiting for Rami. Walks are very important to Bokie, our three-year-old golden retriever who is named after our first dog. This Bokie has his own unique personality, and we all adore him. Of our three goldens, this one seems the most attached to being inside our home with the rest of us. He goes to great pains to be invited inside, including somehow learning not to greet the car when we return on a rainy day. This way, he can keep his feet dry in case we might invite him in. At night he leans against the door so strongly that when we open it in the morning he falls inside.

Each morning for the three years since we've had Bokie, we've taken him for a walk. He is a very affectionate dog, and each of us receives great delight from petting him and watching his silly clumsy ways. Bokie is an integral part of our family.

After putting on rain clothes, I opened the front door fully expecting Bokie to fall inside as usual. No big brown body filled the entrance way. I stepped outside and called, but no wiggly dog greeted me. I knew something was wrong. I checked the garage as once he had been locked in there. No luck! I checked everything that could hold him in. Still no Bokie. I began walking and calling up and down each trail near our house. Not a sign of Bokie!

The Risk To Embrace Pain   151

I went back and called Barry and burst into tears when I heard his voice. I feel so safe with Barry that any hidden emotion quickly comes to the surface. Barry was concerned too, as was Rami. Bokie's absence was so totally unprecedented that I feared the worst. Just two weeks earlier, Barry and I had to call the owners of a dog we found dead on Freedom Boulevard, the major thoroughfare just one half mile from our home. It was not uncommon to see a dead dog, cat or wildlife creature in a ditch along the road. It was also upsetting to me to realize that we had recently taken off his identification collar as we were experimenting with a new electronic flea collar. Bokie was lost with no identification on the stormiest day of the year! I kept picturing him lying in a ditch someplace, hurt and without help. My heart felt like breaking.

I looked over at our Christmas tree. I remembered that just two hours before I had felt for certain I had found my lost Christmas joy. But that was just a memory as I now felt filled with sorrow. Tears welled up in my eyes as I remembered the enthusiasm I had been feeling...so close and now so far away! Happiness seemed far beyond my reach as I grieved over the loss of Bokie.

As the rain pelted down, Rami and I spent several hours driving up and down Freedom Boulevard looking for Bokie in the ditches. Finally we gave up and went home. We walked down to our neighbor Marie and described our sad situation. She gave us hope by telling us Bokie might return in a few days. She thought he might be running after a dog in heat. I felt somewhat better, but still rather sad and fearful for Bokie's life.

Barry and Mira came home and we sat around the table watching the rain and windstorm while working silently on the teddy bears. Barry bolted on the arms and legs, which Mira had previously stuffed. Rami sewed and I embroidered the faces. This project, which had brought so much happiness before, was only filling in the time now. Rami broke the silence by remarking, "I feel as if one of us has just died." We looked around at each other and realized we all shared that feeling.

None of us slept well that night. Santa Cruz storms can be quite severe and this was one of the worst. We moved the girls' mattresses into our bedroom. Throughout the night we took turns checking the front door for the familiar brown form that usually occupied the little mat. Each would return and sadly report to the others, "No Bokie."

Risk To Be Healed

I rose at 4 a.m., got dressed and sat by our Christmas tree to meditate. I looked lovingly at my picture of Mother Mary, a picture I'd been using in my Christmas preparation. I spoke out loud, knowing that our Mother God could hear me and would help me in my hour of sorrow.

"Why do I seem to suffer at Christmas? Why has sickness come to me only in December? Why did we discover our baby had died right at Christmas? Will I ever find the Christmas joy?"

A warmth filled my heart and the answers seemed to flood my being. "Pain comes to you at Christmas to teach you about the inner joy of the season. You suffer because you try to reject the pain in your search for the joy. Pain is a partner to joy and enhances its beauty, like the night enhances the beauty of the day. Christmas comes at the darkest time of the year, bringing with it the light. As you embrace the darkness of life, so much greater will be your joy."

I looked at the lights on the Christmas tree. They glowed so much more beautifully in the darkness. I thought of Bokie and realized I might never see him again. I might never gaze into his warm brown eyes or feel his paw of friendship upon my lap. I embraced the pain of that realization with all the love of my being. As I made that heartache a friend, a teacher to me, joy began to return. Only this time joy was a deeper experience than yesterday when I had danced wildly around the tree. This time joy was in balance with pain. This time I was able to accept not just the pain of losing Bokie, but all the pain I experience in the human condition. The more I accepted and embraced my human suffering, the more joy I felt. I felt the pain and joy that Mary must have felt in giving birth to Jesus, and the pain and joy in Jesus when he realized his mission upon this earth. I thought of the pain and joy that all great souls must have experienced in leaving their heavenly condition to be born upon the earth. In those moments by our tree, I knew I had found my "lost Christmas joy." I realized it was there all the time waiting to be experienced...by embracing the darkness as well as the light in my life.

Instinctively, I went to the front door. Still no Bokie, but now it was OK. I could accept this pain as part of my joy. Even my most joyful childhood moments during Christmas could not equal the joy I felt in that moment...the joy of being in balance with life's pain.

The greater the difficulties the greater also our possibilities.

THE MOTHER (SRI AUROBINDO ASHRAM)

When Barry and the girls awoke they immediately sensed the change in me, which helped them feel more at peace. We spent that day with trust and surrender...and a deeper awareness of the true Christmas spirit.

AUTHOR'S NOTE: Bokie returned to us just before Christmas Eve. Even though he was wet and muddy, the whole family welcomed him with hugs and kisses.

CHAPTER 10

Commitment To Be Healed

You will have wonderful surges forward. Then there must be a time of consolidating before the next forward surge. Accept this as part of the process and never become downhearted.

EILEEN CADDY

BARRY AND I WERE WALKING across the large dining room of a retreat center. From a distant corner someone waved. Barry waved back and then poked me saying, "Wave at that person. I don't know his name but we know him." I eagerly waved, not knowing who it was.

This kind of scene, though quite unusual to some, is quite common to me. I have been very near-sighted since the age of nine. Since graduating from college, I decided I would not be totally dependent upon my glasses. I put them in a case and use them only when absolutely necessary. I am quite comfortable in most situations, except when I cannot recognize people at a distance. Occasionally, I am accused of being unfriendly when really it is just my poor vision.

One close friend had recently purchased contact lenses and urged me to do the same. I knew I needed to make a change. My vision had become much weaker, and I was needing my glasses more and more. I contemplated getting contact lenses and realized I did not want an artificial device for seeing. I wanted to see on my own!

I started to pray each evening and morning for my vision to

improve. I thought I had full faith that God would heal my eyesight, but after two months of prayer my vision remained the same. I was just beginning to doubt that I could be healed when an answer came.

While spreading out our books and tapes at the beginning of a workshop, a man shyly asked if he could place his fliers on the table. "Sure," I said, as I casually picked one up. I read with great interest, "Loving Your Eyes: A Four-Week Course on Vision Improvement." My inner voice said, "This is the answer to your prayer."

Four days later I sat with nine other people as we began our "vision quest". Our teacher, the man we had met at our workshop, was young, enthusiastic, and had healed his own eyes from a twenty-year period of wearing thick glasses. He was challenging us all to do the same. We were excited about the challenge.

Each of us was required to do at least one hour of eye exercises each day for four weeks, attend four weekly group sessions, and attend four weekly private therapy sessions in which we dealt with emotional areas concerning our eyesight.

Driving home that night with my packet of exercises I was excited and yet concerned about the lengthy time commitment. I then remembered my prayer for the healing of my vision and realized this was the form the healing was taking. I, in turn, needed to make the time commitment towards my own healing. I had been praying for a miracle, that my vision would simply improve on its own. God was now asking me to work for this healing. By the time I arrived home I was convinced. I was fully committed to healing my eyes.

The next morning I began rolling my eyes, wearing an eye patch and focusing on different beads on a string. The whole family gathered around in fascination. "This is fun!" I thought. But after several days the novelty wore off. I learned that the commitment to heal can sometimes be very tedious, requiring us to do the same thing over and over.

After two weeks there was no improvement. I was out running on the beach when I saw someone in the distance waving as he ran towards me. I had no idea who it was. I kept running, figuring that person was waving at someone else. Suddenly the man was upon me and grabbed me in a big loving hug. It was our friend John Astin. Smiling, he said, "You didn't know who I was! Maybe you should get a nice pair of contact lenses like me. It's so easy!"

Within minutes we were off jogging in our two separate directions. His words echoed in my head, "It's so easy!" Doubt engulfed me like a dark cloud. Here I had been doing these exercises for two weeks and there was no change. I had been nearsighted for thirty-three years, and my eyes were getting a little weaker each year. Perhaps this is the way it would always be. Perhaps I would never see well. Perhaps healing would take another thirty-three years. That day I didn't do my eye exercises and I didn't practice the suggestions for improved sight. I put on my glasses and resigned myself to always have a weakness of vision. That was a very sad day for me!

The next day I had my private therapy session with my teacher. I told him of my doubt. He asked me to look at all the ways I doubt myself. I soon saw that the doubt about my ability to heal my eyes was connected to other areas of doubt in my life. I realized with a sickening feeling that I was doubting God's ability to heal me. I reflected on the many times I had guided people in their relationships, absolutely convinced that God would heal them. Here was this nice young man, my eye teacher, telling me to do my exercises and trust in God — and I was doubting. As I had seen my own and many other relationships healed, he had seen his own and many other people's vision healed.

Through the experience of feeling doubt about healing my eyes, I had great empathy for those people who doubt that their relationships will ever be beautiful. It is the element of doubt that I, and all people who are seeking healing, must overcome.

I knew that I was needing to actively invite God into my daily eye practice, to ask that the Presence of the Great Healer be with me, helping me to overcome doubt as well as healing my eyes. My daily practice became as important to me as my meditation time. As my eyes ran up and down the string of beads for the one hundredth time, I asked God to be with me and give me greater faith.

The very next day I had my first flash of clear vision. It only lasted a few seconds, but in those few seconds I was able to glimpse a life of perfect vision. Gradually the flashes lasted longer and came more frequently. By the end of the four-week class my daytime vision had definitely improved. I felt empowered and strengthened. I had participated, with God, in a healing experiment. In the last class, our teacher asked us to talk to our eyes and then switch positions and let our eyes talk to us. As I did this I began to cry. My eyes were telling me that their only desire was to serve me. They worked hard at their function of seeing every day. They were doing the best they could and were thankful that finally I was giving them the time and energy to be strengthened so that they could serve me even better. When we switched positions again I felt as if my eyes were like my children asking for love, attention and healing. I felt how much I wanted to give this to them. As I participated in healing my body, I was healing myself, bringing in more strength, trust and confidence in God. Through my tears I saw that healing my eyes was not the work of only four weeks. It required a full commitment without time limits. I knew I did not want to stop. Healing my eyes was a vehicle I could use to attain greater faith.

Over the next month I continued to do my eye exercises. My eyes felt stronger and healthier. Though I had still not reached my goal of being able to recognize people from across a large room, I was growing content and happy with the vision improvement I had received. I was tempted to give up the exercises. I knew I had not gone as far as I could in the healing, yet I was feeling so much better with my vision that I felt like stopping.

The temptation to stop part way through the healing process is a trap for many people. The crisis is over. Things feel better than before. It seems easier and more comfortable to just stop. Contentment, however, does not necessarily mean that healing has been completed. Full healing of a particular situation comes when we are willing to risk going through all the layers of doubt, resistance, fear, pain and sadness. Only then will we find the gift of the experience, the shining treasure of wisdom, understanding and joy. This treasure will then become a great strength in our life and a gift to the world.

Those on the spiritual path can also fall into the trap of giving up part way towards their goal. At first, the desire for God can be very strongly felt. Any sacrifice is gladly endured to reach the goal of love. As we then grow and awaken in our hearts, we learn to use the power of God to create a good life. We can often become comfortable and secure. And contentment can lead to laziness. It can feel so good to have reached some degree of God consciousness that we feel like just staying there. But God, our Higher Self, is constantly urging us onward, to open our heart more, to serve more, to bring even more light into our life. This is the challenge and the commitment of the spiritual life — and of the healing process as well. Do we go part way or all of the way to complete healing and wholeness?

The commitment to heal was so beautifully illustrated in one of our workshops. I shared with the group my own process of beginning to heal my eyes and the commitment that was necessary. People shared their own experiences. Barry asked if there was one more person who would like to share. A hand in the back hesitantly went up and then quickly went down. With my improved vision I instantly detected the source of that hand. "Yes," I said, rather proud of my new ability to see. A woman came forward reluctantly. "My son died eleven years ago," she began, "and I finally feel acceptance of his death. However, the healing is not complete as I have never told anyone how he died. I feel for certain that if I tell anyone, they will hate me."

The woman looked at the floor and was silent. The entire group moved forward slightly in quiet support. Cautiously she looked up and began, "I have been working every day for eleven years to heal from the experience of my son's death. I know that the biggest stumbling block is my fear of telling people. When I heard about this workshop, I knew I had to come."

We encouraged her to share her story about her son's death. When she was ready, she slowly began, "When I was in my early twenties, my husband and I joined what I now know was a cult with a very charismatic and powerful leader. This man promised complete salvation if we followed exactly what he said. The people in the group almost worshipped him and did whatever he said. There was much good and truth to his message but there were also strange directions which we didn't understand. He felt women and children should be strictly subservient to the men and needed to be beaten when they weren't. I myself was beaten once until I was black and blue all over. I accepted this blindly since I wanted the salvation that he promised.

"Because of my husband's work, we were forced to move away from this leader and the group. In a different state we made a new life and our son was born. I felt much happiness in motherhood. I soon forgot about the group, its leader and the strange ways.

"When our son was one and a half years old, I answered the door one day and found the cult leader waiting outside. When I first glanced at him, a feeling of terror passed through me and I clung to our son. He came in and announced that we needed to come back to the group. I started to resist and then remembered the beating. Within a few days he had convinced us to sell everything and return with him.

"Traveling back in the car, I started playing a little game with my son. I would ask, 'Where is your nose? Where is your ear? Where is your tummy?' Each time he would point I would tickle him there. Then I said, 'Where is your belly button?' He giggled and refused to show me. I thought this was very funny until the leader said that our son must be forced to obey. When I tried to force him, he got scared and wouldn't play anymore. The leader said he should be spanked and then deprived of food until he obeyed. Hungry and too scared to respond, our baby was immobilized.

"When we arrived at the leader's home, he ordered us to go out to dinner while he watched our baby. I felt awful, but lacked the courage to stand up to this crazed man. While we were away he tried to get our child to obey him. When it didn't work, the leader started beating him. By the time we arrived home our son was dead, lying in a small heap on the floor."

The woman paused in her story to wipe her eyes. I noticed that everyone in the room was crying. Personally, I felt that I had never heard such a painful story. I prayed that God would show me the beauty through this pain.

The woman continued, "My husband and I took our dead baby to the hospital and they immediately put us both in jail. The leader was also taken to jail. Because no one had the courage to testify against him, he was released. I was given a one-and-a-half-year jail sentence. I cried for a long time, hoping for the release of the pain. Eventually the acute pain subsided, but the shame and guilt have constantly been with me. I know I could have protected my baby if only I had listened to my feelings."

Barry asked her to look at the group. Through tear-filled eyes, each person was showing compassion and understanding. The feeling of forgiveness was very evident in the room. We asked the woman to close her eyes and picture her son. She told us that she has been unable to feel her son since his death. Her constant image is the nightmare of his crumpled and beaten body. We asked each person to use their love and forgiveness to form a bridge of light, helping to unite mother with son. We sat in silence while John Astin, our musician, sang, "I forgive, I forgive, and I love you as you are."

Gradually the woman's face brightened as she felt her son's forgiveness and love for her. She could feel him as a radiant and vast being in the heaven world, rather than a crumpled, beaten little body. Then she said, "His forgiveness for me is very great. Now he is asking me to be as great in my forgiveness."

She then turned that power of forgiveness upon herself. Her face showed inspiration and determination as she said, "I have known for some time that I will be writing about my experience. Now I know I will be writing without bitterness or blame. By so doing, I may be able to help others and may even be able to save a few precious lives."

For eleven years this woman had worked on healing this situation. She had gone through many layers to the place of relative acceptance and peace. Knowing she was unfinished, she dove right into her worst fear and sought the forgiveness she was needing. The experience of her son's death may continue to bring pain to her heart, but now she has begun transforming the experience into a wellspring of forgiveness. The power of her forgiveness will be one of her gifts to the world. And all this because she had the courage to persevere in her healing process.

As this woman and I were hugging each other good bye, she looked at me intently and said, "I have healed my eyes. I no longer wear glasses. You will come to plateaus during your healing journey and will be tempted to give up, but go all the way and reach your goal. The resulting feeling of faith and trust in God is worth every effort."

We smiled at each other in mutual understanding.

The rung of a ladder was never meant to rest upon,
but only to hold your foot long enough to enable you
to put the other foot somewhat higher.

THOMAS HENRY HUXLEY

CHAPTER 11

Taking A Risk
With Your Child

S PARENTS, we need to constantly listen to our hearts as to how to raise our child. Each child comes with his or her own unique set of instructions. It would be nice to have them as a handy computer printout for each day, week or month, but these instructions need to be felt intuitively. We need to listen within our hearts as well as to our child's spoken and unspoken communications, if we want to make decisions which reflect that child's true needs. Sometimes we are asked to raise our children conventionally and at other times we are asked to be pioneers. The risk comes not only with our listening and feeling but also with our willingness to trust what we hear and feel.

When our oldest daughter Rami was finishing the third grade at a local Waldorf school, it became apparent to us that she needed and wanted to be home more. It was a very difficult decision to take her out of a well-established school and let her stay home.

Academic education was very important during my childhood. I received much approval from my parents for good grades in school. My father spent long and patient hours each night helping my brother and me with our homework.

Once at home, Rami had little interest in academics, but threw herself wholeheartedly into creative play and discovering nature. She climbed trees with a passion, spending long hours feeling the movement of the branches, singing to the birds, and sensing the strength of each tree. She made hidden houses and delightful restaurants where strawberry tea was served in a mint leaf. With great enthusiasm she explored the woods and countryside around our house. Rainy days found her producing volumes of art work.

Meanwhile, I poured over books on homeschooling. I tried to present lessons in math and reading in an interesting way. Rami tolerated these lessons with a quiet politeness, one eye always on the great outdoors, and trying hard to stay awake. Because of my own academic upbringing, worrisome thoughts would pop up in my mind from time to time.

We tested Rami and found her to be far below grade-level in all subjects. So we found a wonderful tutor who brought her reading up to standard, but intellectual learning just didn't hold much interest for her. Rami's world largely consisted of listening to nature, watching things grow, learning about the American Indians, looking for fairies and gnomes, and feeling the angels. She was extremely happy in her life and glowed with an inner radiance. When I could still my mind, I felt very peaceful about Rami. The time at home and in nature was obviously fulfilling a great need in her. Her happiness in life was only disturbed when my mind got the better of me and I began to worry about her academic success. Then I would push her to learn more and we would both become unhappy.

Rami's lack of interest in academics was a source of worry for both Barry and me, but especially me. I had great difficulty letting go of the concept that a happy, well adjusted child also meant doing well academically. I kept thinking that I was failing Rami, that her life was in some way going to be damaged. In my meditation, I asked again and again for reassurance that letting her stay home was the right thing. In peaceful moments I received beautiful assurance which would last a few days. Then my mind would take over again.

Finally, in a moment of panic, I enrolled Rami in an academic setting for school and was determined that she go. I presented the idea to her gently. She pondered my words and then went out to sit in her favorite tree. Not wanting to disturb her, I decided to go for a walk by myself along our country road. Suddenly Rami came bounding along beside me, her long legs making her look like a deer. Her blonde hair flew in the breeze and she had a look of absolute peace and inspiration. She spoke each word slowly and with determination.

"I need to stay home some more. There is something else I am needing to do here."

She did not know what that something was, but she knew it was special. There was no need arguing with that look of determination. My plans for her academic success vanished and her plan for "something special" began to unfold.

A short time later, my worry and concern for Rami took its last strong stand. I had entered a restroom filled with girls Rami's age, all laughing and brushing their hair. "I bet those girls are getting good grades," I wistfully thought. "Perhaps Rami will never do well in academics," I sadly thought. As I started to brush my hair, sharing the mirror with the group of pre-teen girls, I felt a beautiful mother presence beside me. Her beautiful words filled me:

"Rami has a gift to give to the world. She cannot learn to read, spell or do math properly until that gift is given. Right now the gift is much more important than facts. Trying to fill her mind will only cloud the clarity of her gift. Trust in her wisdom to stay home one more year and let go of the push for mental learning."

Rami was now almost two grade levels below average. I would like to say I stopped worrying altogether after receiving such a beautiful assurance...but I didn't. My worry was at a minimal level, however, and I stopped pushing Rami. As soon as I stopped putting pressure on her, she began to realize that what she had wanted was to write a book. This book, which eventually became *Rami's Book: The Inner Life Of A Child*, was the main focus for her third year at home. Barry and I helped with spelling and sentence structure, but the ideas and creativity were entirely hers. All that she had been learning by herself the two previous years at home while out among the grasses and trees became of vital importance. Rami had been learning to listen and receive, and now she began listening and receiving her book. Excitement grew in our house as chapter after wonderful chapter was completed. Beautiful color art work piled up by her desk.

Rami worked with certainty and purpose. I was beginning to understand the importance of our risk to keep her home and let go of the academic push in her life. Rami was fulfilling a part of her destiny on earth. The whole family thrilled with the energy coming through her. I would have suspected that little sister Mira might have been jealous at all the attention we were giving to Rami's book, but Mira was more thrilled than any of us. She sat by the hour encouraging and supporting Rami.

When Rami had completed her book, Barry and I were faced with a financial risk. To publish the book in color, in a tasteful and professional way, would mean using every penny, if not more, from our savings. The printer's estimate of twenty thousand dollars was staggering. We could change from color to black and white, and go with cheaper paper, cover and binding to make the book affordable to us. Without much hesitation we decided to risk all of our savings to produce *Rami's Book* into the most beautiful gift we could give to the world.

The response to *Rami's Book* has gone beyond what we could have ever suspected. Adults are reading and studying the book to rediscover their own childhood. Children are listening to her words and stories with great eagerness. Parents report that their children will listen to Rami more so than to an adult author. They feel a special relationship with a child like themselves.

Barry and I, of course, almost burst with pride whenever someone writes to us about how *Rami's Book* has helped them. Her writing has even been selected over ours by a major magazine. The pride and joy we feel in her gift goes beyond her accomplishment. We feel a joy in ourselves that we were able to take the risk and allow Rami a different type of education for three years. We allowed her to be different from the norm, and to learn in her own way.

Soon after *Rami's Book* was completed, Rami began picking up books and reading on her own. Writing the book sparked her interest in reading. With the book completed, her mind opened to learning, and she could hardly get enough. I wondered what the next step would be.

A short time later, a talented young woman approached me after church and said, "I have been feeling that I would really like Rami to be in my sixth grade class in public school. I know she could be in seventh grade, but I think the sixth grade experience at the middle school would be good for her."

As she described her teaching style, I knew this was the next step for Rami. She entered school once again with the same zeal that she had for climbing trees. Soon she was on the honor roll and later was voted "student of the month."

Is there a risk you are needing to take with your child? Is your heart directing you to go in a certain direction with your child, but your practical, conventional mind is resisting? We need to always remember that our children have much greater parents than we can ever be for them. The wisdom of our Mother/Father God will speak to us in our hearts helping us to guide our children until they can properly guide themselves. What had bothered us the most about our risk with Rami was that we could not see the whole picture, we could not imagine the gift that would come of the experience. We had to constantly renew our faith and trust in God, and affirm that Rami was being totally loved and cared for by a source much greater than our own personal parenting skills.

The risk with your children may not have anything to do with school, but it may involve something to help bring out their unique and special qualities. Listen to your own inner guidance and the needs of your children. Then take a leap of faith. Our children are each special and individual. When we free them to express their uniqueness, their gifts to the world can pour forth.

The earth is our Mother,
She gives us food.
The sun is our Father,
He gives us warm light.
The stars are all our brothers and sisters,
and the moon guides us along.

So don't you know how lucky you are,
to have so many friends.

The earth is loving you,
the sun is loving you,
the stars are loving you,
and the moon is loving you.

So don't you know how much you are loved.

FROM *RAMI'S BOOK: THE INNER LIFE OF A CHILD*

CHAPTER 12

The Risk to Serve

MAGINE YOURSELF IN A RADIANT WORLD right before taking birth into this present life. With you, at this moment of power, are those beings of light who will be helping you as you live your life. You know that by learning the lessons of physical life on earth, you will be able to grow closer to your Source, the beautiful center of love and light. You can look upon your life and see the opportunities and spiritual lessons that await you. You feel tremendous gratitude for the life that is before you. At this moment you are given final instructions for your new life. You are told to love others, serve others and to remember your beautiful source, your true heaven home. Then, just before you enter life in an infant body, you vow to use this life to love, serve and remember.

Each of us made a similar vow. All of us have within us the memory, determination and momentum of this powerful declaration. It is the deepest desire of each person to fulfill this vow. In the moment of making the vow, we are each shown the tremendous help and power that is available to us. Loving, serving and remembering God are essential parts of who we are. Each time we tap into one of the elements of our vow, we are tapping into our source and the very meaning of our existence.

Whenever we desire to truly love and serve, we only need to remember our Source and the beautiful light-workers who are waiting to pour the light through us. We will always be given the power to heal and to bless. The risk of loving and serving is to have full confidence and faith that God is with us.

Last winter we were asked to give a talk to a Unity Church which was a two-hour drive from our home. We decided to make a day of it and take Rami and Mira to the Exploratorium in San Francisco. The church, we figured, was just a short hop over the Oakland Bay Bridge.

As we left that day I felt myself beginning to get the flu. I tried to ignore it. We had a great time at the Exploritorium and, at 4:30 p.m., decided to drive over the bridge so we would have plenty of time to prepare for the talk at 7:00 p.m. Coming from the country, we forget the ways of a big city. The bridge was packed with cars moving at a snail's pace. We had our motorhome which was difficult to drive at that stop and go pace. Two hours later we were still on the bridge. Tension was mounting in our camper. Barry had a big headache, I had given in to the feeling of the flu and the girls were hungry. I was driving and pulled off the road abruptly as I felt sick. Not used to driving a motorhome, I pulled right into a road sign. C R U N C H ... the sound of metal against metal was deafening. Barry was upset with me, I felt worse, and the girls were crying.

This is how we arrived at the Unity Church to give our talk. As we were late, our dear friend and musician John Astin was already covering for us. He was singing his heart out, secretly hoping that we would come soon. The church was small and very crowded. Our half-hour-late arrival was noticed by all as we crept up to our front row seats. I had never felt more ill-prepared to give a talk.

The minister stood up to introduce us. She gave one of the most beautiful and lengthy introductions we had ever received. As she was praising us I thought grimly, "She'll be disappointed when she finds out the two people she is introducing aren't here tonight."

I wanted to run from the room, rather than stay and risk disappointing everyone. Would people stand up and leave in the middle?

Would they yawn and show their displeasure? Do people ever throw rotten vegetables when a speaker isn't very good?

I glanced at Rami and Mira who had wanted to come for the beginning part of the talk. They looked worried! They had seen Mama and Daddy give many talks before. They knew what a hard time we were having in that moment, which contrasted sharply with our usual smiles of confidence. Rami leaned over and comforted me, "I'll say a prayer for you, Mama. I'll tell Mira to do the same."

Both girls closed their eyes in faithful prayer. I glanced at Barry. A smile passed between us at last. We looked at the girls sweetly praying for their parents and then we remembered. With the praises of the minister still filling the air, we remembered our Source. For a brief moment we re-experienced our vow and remembered the great light and power that is available to us all, if we will but humble ourselves to ask and receive. In our present state of consciousness, still feeling like we were back in the bumper-to-bumper traffic with headache, flu and tension, we felt powerless to talk to anyone. Yet our risk was to pray, tap into our Source of power and have full faith that we would receive the necessary help.

Applause filled the church and with a bolt of energy I didn't even think I had, I sprung to the microphone with Barry. It turned out to be one of the best talks we'd ever given. Because we had felt incapable of giving the talk, we had leaned totally on God and, as always, the light had come through.

Throughout each day, we are all being given inner promptings on ways to heal and serve others. Out of shyness, lack of confidence in God, or doubt, we let these opportunities slip by. Each time this happens, however, we are also letting go of a chance to have the healing light of God pass through us...a chance to be healed ourselves.

Recently I was on retreat in Big Sur writing for this book. On one particular day of my five day stay, a friend was also on retreat. She too had come to write, to have time away from family responsibilities, to be totally alone, and center her thoughts on God.

During the afternoon of her stay, I had left the retreat housing and had walked down the road hoping to sit at a particular bench which had a lovely view of the canyon. I had paper and pen and was determined to finish my chapter. As I approached this bench I noticed a man was already there. Trying not to feel disappointed that my favorite place was taken, I rationalized that I'd walk the extra half mile to the next bench. But as I passed by the bench my inner voice prompted me, "Sit next to that man and tell him he is loved."

"I can't do that," my mind argued. "It is an act of courtesy here to leave people alone on their retreats."

"That man is needing help." My inner voice was a little stronger, but I rationalized that he might not want me to come to him and that I had a lot of my own work to do. Yet it was really my shyness and fear of taking the risk that caused me to walk on down the road to the other bench. Strangely, I was unable to write very much.

Walking back up the road I again came to the first bench. My friend was just walking away. The man waved and smiled at her as she left. Her face was radiant! Breaking my silence, I asked her to tell me what had just happened. She related that as she was walking down the road her inner voice prompted her to sit next to the man. She said that she felt rather foolish as she walked towards him, but went anyway. She found him crying softly. His wife and child had recently died in a car crash and he felt alone and depressed. He had driven up the road to the retreat out of desperation. He felt like taking his own life. My friend confided how she had comforted him. As she put her hand on his shoulder, he relaxed and opened to her words. They spent over an hour together. She looked so beautiful and recharged with light. As we approached her room she smiled and said, "I feel so filled with inspiration, I can hardly wait to start my writing."

My own blank pages lay on the desk that day as I reflected on the risk involved in serving others. The inner promptings to give strength and healing to our human and animal brothers and sisters come each day. As we take the risk of appearing foolish or out of place, we are given a great blessing in return.

When our heart gives a prompting to heal and serve others, there is no punishment for walking away. We are simply walking away from a mutual blessing. Look for many opportunities to give strength, appreciation or comfort in your lives. You will be blessed each time you choose to serve.

Sometimes the inner voice will prompt us to do something that doesn't make sense to our rational mind. During a workshop in our home, a woman who had been a nun and had recently left her order was expressing her difficulty relating to the world. "Something seems lacking in my interactions with others," she explained. Members of the group were comforting her and offering suggestions on how to deepen communication. I was sitting quietly, praying for help when an inner prompting came, "Go get Rami's baby doll."

You would have to see that baby doll to know how ridiculous the idea sounded to me. Rami had received the doll when she was one year old. The hair was pulled out, the eyes punched in, the skin darkened from dirt and the head wobbly from falling off several times. I ignored the prompting, and began thinking of an appropriate communication exercise she could do with the group.

The woman started to cry and shared her hopelessness. "I have been to communication classes and have sincerely tried to deepen myself, but something remains unhealed."

"Go get Rami's baby doll," the prompting came again. As casually as I could, I got up and went into Rami's room. I tried to be quiet, but still made noise as I rummaged in her closet for the doll. "Baby doll" looked worse than I had remembered.

"Now put diapers and baby pajamas on her," the inner voice continued. I crossed through the group of people again and now rummaged through another closet for the old diapers and pajamas. Several people looked at me with curiosity. That task completed, I was then told to wrap the doll in a soft baby blanket.

"Now place the doll gently in her arms," I was inwardly told. As I did so, the woman held the baby close to her heart and her crying deepened. Through her tears she shared, "I have yearned for a baby ever since childhood. In the convent I had convinced myself that I did not want to be a mother. I have avoided looking at children, babies and mothers." Holding the old baby doll she was able to release her secret longing. Her healing came through accepting her desire to be a mother.

Later I held the baby doll to my own heart. She didn't look so bad now. The diapers had fluffed her up a bit, and the pajamas covered up much of the dirt. The blanket hid her bald spot and steadied her wobbly head. I felt grateful for the doll and more grateful that I had had the courage to listen.

Behind every inner prompting to serve and heal is the help and full power of the great beings of light who are continually available to assist us. As we take the risk to offer healing, we are expressing our faith and confidence that God will heal through us. We are all needed in the healing service to humanity. We simply need to humble ourselves and ask for the help and guidance.

Sometimes healing comes through sitting quietly and sending out light and love to our fellow humans or world conditions. Sometimes healing is given through physical touch or the spoken word. Every effort on our part is always backed with the strength of the Great Light. As we endeavor to love, serve and remember we fulfill our original vow and purpose for this life. As our willingness increases, so also does our sense of fulfillment in life. As we remember, recognize and honor the Source of all true healing and allow that power to come through us, we are healed ourselves. As we sow seeds of love and healing to others, so also will we receive. As we strive to help another of God's children, we find that we also have been helped. Eventually we realize that we can never reach our own goal until we are ready to help another reach theirs. We cannot be healed until we take the risk to heal another. The risk to heal another of God's children is an essential part of the risk to be healed.

Love everyone. Serve everyone. Remember God.

NEEM KAROLI BABA

Sarah, a woman in her fifties, had been sitting at the outside of the group looking somewhat disinterested. I beckoned her to come to the center.

We asked Sarah why she had come to our retreat. She told a story of a chaotic and abusive childhood, and then concluded, "I have never really wanted to be alive!"

It was an intense moment for everyone in the room, as each of us was forced to reflect on our own resistance to life. It then occurred to me that Sarah needed the experience of being welcomed into the world with loving arms. With her permission, we formed a living womb by sitting closely around her. We asked her to close her eyes and wrap her arms around herself, holding the image of being in a womb. When she had gotten accustomed to that position, we then asked her to start tightening her arms and hold the image of a contracting uterus.

"Are you ready to come out into the world?", we asked.

"No," was the muffled reply.

"OK, then squeeze harder until you feel ready."

"Now I'm ready," she gasped through squeezing arms.

"Good," we coached. "Start the process of unfolding and opening into your birth."

While the group continued singing to her, Sarah began to unfold muscle by muscle. We all watched expectantly as she timidly opened her eyes and looked at the group. We then sang a sweet song to welcome her into the world. We greeted her with moist eyes and loving smiles. Feeling all this love directed towards her, she began to cry. Then she started laughing. A camera flashed and someone spoke, "We have to have baby pictures." Sarah did indeed look like a newborn baby, content and happy for the first time in her life, as she later told us.

Then another woman in her thirties spoke up. She was very moved by the whole experience. She looked at Sarah and said, "I feel like I have also been resisting life. I can't remember ever being wanted by my parents." Tears were flowing down her cheeks.

I knew in that moment there was only one place for this woman to be. I asked Sarah if she would make her lap available for this woman. I knew that Sarah, in her "newborn condition," could have been loved and held for a long time, which might have been fine. I also knew that in her open and receptive condition she could be used as a powerful instrument of healing for another.

She answered the question by sitting upright without hesitation and reaching out her arms toward the younger woman, who then came, lay down in her lap and let her tears be released. Sarah stroked this woman's head and spoke tender, healing words of encouragement.

It was a powerful moment for all of us. That day, we more deeply understood a fundamental truth of healing. We saw that Sarah's rebirth experience was only part of her healing, part of her risk to be healed. Her taking the risk to heal another brought more depth and completion to her own personal healing. Her first risk was to receive, and her second risk was to let go of that heavenly receptive state in order to give to another. In her risk to lose that precious gift of contented peace, she found that she had gained even more: the deeper peace of serving God through serving another human being. Two were healed instead of one.

That evening Sarah made a joyous vow. "I vow," she triumphantly said, "to live life to the fullest!" The room shook with applause.

Whenever it feels appropriate during a workshop or retreat, we lead a "parent-child practice." Sometimes we divide the participants into two groups standing on either side of the room with each group having an equal number of men and women. One group is designated the "children" and the other the "parents." The "children" are then asked to scan the "parents" to pick out one parent with whom it would be a healing risk to pair up, perhaps someone who possessed a quality of one of their own parents, a quality with which they had some difficulty. After all the "children" have made their choices they cross the room together to pick out their "parents."

We then instruct the "parents" to take their child (or children as the case may be) and sit down together. When we were first experimenting with this practice, we had parent and child sit facing each other, communicating with words. It just didn't have the power. Verbalizing these sometimes highly charged, emotion-filled issues all too often activated the left brain, where they were then intellectually discussed.

So we had to modify the practice. We had the parents sit with their child's head on their lap without any talking. The "children" are asked to let go of their adult bodies and consciousness and to feel the little child within them, the child who simply needs to be loved, nourished and protected. We ask the parents to use their hands to gently stroke the heads of their children, and feel that their hands are being overshadowed and used as instruments of light and spirit. Often we are blessed to have either John Astin or Charley and Lori Thweatt (or all three) to sing gentle songs. There is usually a deep release of feeling throughout the room as one person's catharsis catalyzes others. For many it is a profound healing experience.

Now the challenge is ending this part of the practice, regrouping the original groups, and switching roles, so that all those who were children can now be parents and vise-versa. It is a challenge because many of the "children" have worked hard to let go of their "grown-up" consciousness and have become attached to the sweet nurturing and receptivity. So we give a little "pep-talk" about balancing their receiving with giving. We acknowledge that some of the children do not feel complete with being a child, and they feel they might lose something, or close off an experience, by switching to be an adult. And occasionally there are a few children who are so deep in their experiences that we just let them stay where they are. For most of the children, however, it is a wonderful healing experience to then become a parent of someone else. In many cases, the issues they were working through as a child are strikingly similar to the ones their child is now working on. As parents, they have another chance to heal those issues by accepting and blessing them in their child.

Just as in real life, most people never feel completely ready to become parents. Joyce and I, having been together twelve years, still felt there was so much more to heal in ourselves and in our relationship before we would be ready to be parents. We realized we would never learn how to become parents until we became parents. It is a paradox of life. Rami, and then Mira, taught us all we needed to know. Their very presence in our lives brought the growth we were needing. And through loving them we have been loving and healing the child within ourselves.

Many of us have asked, with varying degrees of awareness, to be of service in this world and lifetime, to be a healing force for the planet. There was a time in 1982 when Joyce and I were having a long period of disharmony. Although deeply committed to one another, it was discouraging to be suffering so deeply in our relationship. Finally one morning we meditated together and then prayed to be shown why we were having such a hard time. We received the answer. Months before, in a moment of deep inspiration, we had together asked to be of service to the Light. It was a joyful and yet sobering moment. Then the hard times hit, and it seemed to hit us from all sides, and we forgot that moment of asking. It was our very asking to be light-workers that raised us to a new level of consciousness. Because of that shift, a rearranging had to take place on all levels. The energies within us which were incompatible with the new level, the habits, the karma, the old ways of thinking and relating, became starkly visible, and had to be dealt with.

In addition, we were shown that all of our pain and suffering was preparing us for a deeper work with people in relationship. Hard as it was, Joyce and I needed to experience in our relationship the different kinds of pain and suffering that others experience. These understandings helped us greatly, and shortly thereafter we started writing *The Shared Heart*.

We met a woman once who told us an unforgettable story. As a child in a Nazi concentration camp, she was pinned to the ground under the foot of a guard, and made to watch him machine-gun to death her parents, her brothers and sisters, and all her relatives. Despite the gruesomeness of the scene before her, she prayed with a child's faith and was lifted out of her body and transported to a place that was filled with light. When she came back to her body, she woke up in the arms of the famous author and philosopher, Victor Frankl. A prisoner there at the same time, he took care of her.

Now this woman could have been bitter, resentful, emotionally-crippled, and profoundly depressed by such a trauma. But instead, she was filled with joy, and had one of the most infectious laughs we had ever heard. Her life was dedicated to bringing joy to sick and dying children in the hospital. The depth of her suffering and loss of her family gave her an even deeper longing to serve. She understood pain and suffering better than anyone, and therefore could effortlessly touch with compassion the hearts of others who were in pain.

As we mentioned earlier, Joyce and I have followed with interest the miraculous appearances of Mother Mary in Medjugorge, Yugoslavia. For several years she has been appearing to a small group of children, giving messages through them to many thousands of pilgrims from all over the world who travel there. The miracles and the healings have created an uproar in the scientific as well as religious worlds.

One particular message touched me in a profound way. She asked people to start using their hands to heal and to bless one another. She said it is not necessary to be a healer, or even to know anything about healing. It is only necessary to ask for healing in Her name, in the name of God, in the name of the Light, and all the healing power of the universe will be transmitted through those hands.

In this small town in Eastern Europe, many thousands of people, most with little or no formal education, simple and humble in their thinking, and trusting the words of the mother of the Christ coming out of the mouths of children, are reaching out to touch and heal one another. And just as a stone when tossed into a quiet pond creates expanding, never-ending ripples, people in surrounding towns and cities are reaching out to one another with the touch of peace, taking the risk to overcome social inhibitions, taking the risk to heal. Wherever we travel, we are seeing the same ripple effect. We are so blessed to be living at this time when we can witness the many ripples of love joining together and becoming one great force turning the tide of history...bringing a healing peace to this planet and to all who dwell upon it.

I slept and dreamt that life was joy.
I awoke and saw that life was service.
I acted and behold, service was joy.

RABINDRANATH TAGORE

About the authors:

Joyce and Barry Vissell, a nurse and medical doctor couple since 1968, are the authors of three books: *THE SHARED HEART, MODELS OF LOVE,* and *RISK TO BE HEALED.* They have counseled individuals and couples since 1972, and have traveled internationally conducting talks and workshops on healing, relationship and parenting. Their favorite work is parenting their two daughters, Rami and Mira, in the hills near Santa Cruz, California.

If you would like to be notified of a workshop or event with Barry and Joyce to be held in your area, if you would like to sponsor or organize such an event, or if you would like to share your reactions and feelings about this book (which they welcome), they may be contacted through:

RAMIRA PUBLISHING
P.O.BOX 1707
APTOS, CALIFORNIA 95001

AVAILABLE BOOKS AND TAPES BY THE VISSELLS:

THE SHARED HEART: Relationship Initiations And Celebrations

Going into its sixth printing since being released in 1984, this book has touched the hearts of many thousands. *"...a map of the relationship journey."* — RAM DASS. *"...full to overflowing with immeasurable guidelines on using our relationships as tools for our further awakening."* —SCIENCE OF THOUGHT REVIEW, ENGLAND. *"...celebrates, in all its aspects, LOVE."* —NEWPORT THIS WEEK.

186 pages ISBN 0-9612720-0-7 $9.95

MODELS OF LOVE: The Parent-Child Journey

"...full of miraculous incidents and sacred moments of loving connection that will bring tears to your eyes ... the valuable lessons and insights of MODELS OF LOVE can be appreciated by both parents and non-parents alike, as this book goes straight to the heart and awakens the spirit within us all." —THE WHOLE LIFE MONTHLY.

320 pages ISBN 0-9612720-1-5 $10.95

RISK TO BE HEALED: The Heart of Personal and Relationship Growth

Barry and Joyce's most recent book, filled with stories from their own continuing growth, as well as the healing risks people have taken in their counseling and workshops. The book begins with the profound experience of Anjel's death in utero and her subsequent birth into the lives of the authors. There are chapters on: risk-taking in relationship, the power of right livelihood, healing through the veil, addictions, appreciation, vulnerability, and simplicity.

192 pages ISBN 0-9612720-2-3 $9.95

RAMI'S BOOK: The Inner Life of a Child

"Rami's Book is like a breath of fresh air teaching us about our innocence and the simplicity of loving ourselves and others."
— GERALD JAMPOLSKY, M.D. AND DIANE CIRINCIONE

Rami Vissell wrote and illustrated this book during her eleventh year of life. Through stories and poems, visualizations and practices, and her refreshing full-color artwork, she guides the reader, whether adult or child, to a deeper awareness of the purpose of life ... this book is a celebration of the magical child within each of us.

56 pages, hardcover, ISBN 0-9612720-4-X, $13.95

THE SHARED HEART CASSETTE TAPE: The Relationship Of Love

This is a tape of inspiration and guided visualizations for individuals and couples interested in relationship as a journey of the heart. It captures on tape the essence of *THE SHARED HEART*. Side one is by Barry, side two by Joyce. Gentle background music by Steven Bergman and Charlie Thweatt.

Cassette Tape $9.95

MOTHER-CHILD BONDING DURING PREGNANCY

The foundation of bonding between mother and child occurs before birth —not after. This cassette is a guided journey into the bonding experience —the heart-to-heart connection between mother and baby. Side one guides the mother's hands in a light-touch bonding massage. Side two is a guided meditation helping the mother to feel her true relationship with her child.

Cassette tape $9.95

TRANSITIONS INTO FATHERHOOD: Personal Growth For Expectant Fathers

This tape is a journey to the inner experience of fatherhood. Side one guides men over the various stumbling blocks encountered during pregnancy, culminating in a guided imagery experience of pregnancy for men. Side two includes conscious fathering practices and ends with an inspiring guided meditation journey into fatherhood.

Cassette tape $9.95

A JOURNEY OF LOVE: Couples Moving Into Parenthood

How can couples consciously prepare for the profound changes parenthood will bring to their relationship? This cassette offers inspiration and very practical help in the journey from couplehood to parenthood. Side one includes practices couples can do to cultivate their emerging parenthood. Side two will help the couple toward deeper levels of communication, ending with an inspiring shared visualization which they will want to do together often.

Cassette tape $9.95

WE WOULD LIKE TO MAKE AVAILABLE TO OUR READERS A FEW ITEMS WHICH HAVE HELPED OUR FAMILY

SPIRITUAL TEACHING FOR CHILDREN by Jenny Dent, White Eagle Lodge, England. This is a series of four play-as-you-learn books. Included are: *GOD LOVES US ALL, WHERE IS HEAVEN?, THE GIANT JIGSAW*, and *GREAT TEACHERS*. This is the best children's introduction to universal spiritual truths and meditation that we have found.

Set of four books, $12.95

ANGELS BE WITH YOU by Mark and Nancy Wallace.
Originally produced as a companion to *Models of Love*... A delightful collection of bedtime songs, lullabies and sweet harp music.

Cassette with lyrics included, $9.95

WINGS TO MY HEART by Charley Thweatt and Rosie Lovejoy.
This is a lively and touching recording for children of all ages. We listen to this tape over and over.

Cassette with lyrics included, $9.95

I CLAIM A MIRACLE also by Charley and Rosie.
This recording is filled with joy and heart. We and our children love to sing these songs.

Cassette with lyrics included, $9.95

FOR A CHILD'S HEART by Timmaris and Diane.
An old favorite of our family ... joyful, inspiring and devotional songs for children of all ages.

Cassette, $9.95

INTO THE LIGHT by John Astin
Exquisite, devotional love songs, some upbeat and joyful, others quiet and contemplative; all heart-openers!

Cassette with lyrics included, $9.95

WAKE TO THE BEAUTY by John Astin
John's songs capture the spirit of our workshops and retreats. Beautifully arranged and recorded.

Cassette with lyrics included, $9.95

WINDS OF GRACE by John Astin
John's latest work of art... Songs wonderfully expressing the soul's yearning for the light of God.

Cassette with lyrics included, $9.95

I OFFER YOU MY HEART by Charley and Lori Thweatt
> From tender love songs to wild dance tunes, a captivating recording. Charley and Lori's newest and their first as a couple.
>> Cassette, $9.95

LENINGRAD by Charley Thweatt
> A moving and very powerful tape ... includes many of the songs that have taken our workshops and retreats to deeper levels of love.
>> Cassette, $9.95

VOICES OF THE HEART by Michael (Maitreya) and Maloah Stillwater
> New age choral music with a large choir ... evokes deep feelings of peace. A wonderful sing-along tape.
>> Cassette with lyrics included, $9.95

SHORES OF PARADISE By Maloah and Michael Stillwater
> Gentle sounds of zither, ocean, birds and guitar. One of our favorite tapes for meditation or relaxation.
>> Cassette, $9.95

AWAKER OF HEARTS by Diane Bardwell
> *"If I were to make my own tape, this is the closest to what my heart would want to sing."* —JOYCE VISSELL
>> Cassette, $9.95

SONGS OF THE HEART by Susan McCullen
> Susan's voice and music bathe us in the presence of Divine Mother ... a very healing tape.
>> Cassette, $9.95

ORDERING INFORMATION:

- QUANTITY DISCOUNT: Order any 4 items, get 5th item **FREE**.
(Free item must be book or tape by Vissell; *Rami's Book* not included)
- Shipping: $2.00 first item; $1.00 each additional item
- California residents add 6.5% sales tax
- Send order to:

RAMIRA PUBLISHING
P.O.BOX 1707
APTOS, CA 95001
(408) 429-9311